The Impact of
LARGE LANDOWNERS
on Land Markets

Edited by
Raphael W. Bostic

LINCOLN INSTITUTE
OF LAND POLICY
CAMBRIDGE, MASSACHUSETTS

Library of Congress Cataloging-in-Publication Data
The impact of large landowners on land markets / edited by Raphael W. Bostic.
p. cm.
Includes bibliographical references and index.
ISBN 978-1-55844-189-7
1. Land tenure.   2. Land tenure.   3. Landowners.   I. Bostic, Raphael W.
II. Lincoln Institute of Land Policy.
HD1251.I47 2009
333.3—dc22   2009013040

Designed and typeset by Technologies 'N Typography in Merrimac, Massachusetts.
Printed and bound by Puritan Press in Hollis, New Hampshire.
♻ The paper is Roland Enviro100, an acid-free, 100 percent recycled sheet.

MANUFACTURED IN THE UNITED STATES OF AMERICA

CONTENTS

ILLUSTRATIONS

FIGURES

TABLES

FOREWORD

Rosalind Greenstein

What happens when one owner or one institution has significant control over the local land market? What tensions might this create between public and private interests?

The chapters in this volume examine these issues by looking at large landowners in various contexts. In the United States, for example, the large tracts of land held by private owners are often situated on the fringes of metropolitan areas. Frequently, this land is in transition from agricultural to urban use and represents a source of income or a legacy for the next generation. Many universities own large parcels of land. Because these universities contribute to the urban economy, they often hold the bargaining advantage in comparison with other actors when town-gown issues arise.

In Nigeria, as in much of Africa, a considerable portion of land is held privately, albeit communally. Land ownership and land supply decisions have more to do with family or clan marriages than with the logic of city building.

How do the actions of individual landowners affect our capacity to create cities that work for all? How well can these individual actors balance the competing interests of those living in neighborhoods, towns, cities, and regions? Each chapter in this volume highlights the behaviors of the actors in the land market. Although tensions can arise between the stakeholders during the development process, these tensions are not the problem. Rather, they challenge us and provide an opportunity to shape our cities collectively.

The research supported by the Department of Economic and Community Development at the Lincoln Institute of Land Policy is intended to improve the capacity of such stakeholders to define their own interests in economic and community development as a prelude to entering into effective negotiations that balance the competing interests of the actors. This volume will motivate scholarly and policy efforts to empower the actors to intervene in the land development process.

PREFACE

This volume is the result of a multiyear exploration of the significance of large landowners and their roles in land markets. The project began for me in October 2005 in Kansas City, Missouri, over lunch at the annual meeting of the Association of Collegiate Schools of Planning. Rosalind Greenstein, chair of the Department of Economic and Community Development of the Lincoln Institute of Land Policy, mentioned that the success of the Institute's extended project on universities had led her to wonder whether universities were but one example of a broader class of institutions—large landowners—that could provide real insights into land use and land use policy.

I had just begun research on hospitals (one piece of which is included in this volume), and though neither I nor my coauthors had ever conceived of the project in that way, it was evident that large landholder hospitals were quite important in terms of land use. If this was true in the case of hospitals and universities, perhaps it applied to other large landowners.

A research conference was convened in September 2006 with a diverse set of scholars who had given some thought to the idea of large landowners as a vehicle or tool for study. They addressed how large landowners shape the urban landscape, with a particular focus on how large landowners engage their communities. The chapters in this volume reflect the energy, scope, and insights of the conference.

First and foremost, I would like to acknowledge and thank Rosalind Greenstein for her vision and willingness to explore the landscape of large landowners. I also thank the contributors to this volume, who have devoted great energy, effort, and creativity in designing and conducting their research. I give special thanks to Pengyu Zhu, who came to the project in the eleventh hour and was instrumental in the completion of the volume's first chapter.

Thanks to all the conference participants. I particularly want to thank Christopher Briem, Sabina Deitrick, Dawn Jourdan, Anil Kashyap, Anamaria Martins, Melchior Sawaya Neto, Shashwat Tewary, Piyush Tiwari, and Kimberly Winson-Geideman, who contributed conference papers that were ultimately not included in the volume. Each made important contributions to the conference by highlighting interesting aspects of large landowners, raising questions and issues to be considered, helping advance discussions, and honing our understanding of the roles that large landowners play in land markets.

Finally, I would like to thank the Lincoln Institute of Land Policy staff, and particularly Anne Battis. Their support and guidance helped keep the project moving smoothly and efficiently.

THE IMPACT OF
LARGE LANDOWNERS
ON LAND MARKETS

INTRODUCTION

The study of land use and development is necessarily multidimensional since there are many varied interests that come to bear on the land use outcomes ultimately realized. These interests range from those of public sector officials tasked with delivering services to a diverse community of residents and workers, to those of residents seeking to maximize the local quality of life, to those of businesses seeking to increase their productivity and profits, to those of landowners interested in creating and maintaining value. All these players face significant pressures from both market and social forces, and outcomes are the result of the complex interweaving of these forces.

The research studies compiled in this volume, taken together, provide a strong argument that large landowners represent an ideal group through which to study land use and how these many forces interact and converge to shape outcomes and governance and institutional form. The approach here is to be illustrative, so rather than attempt to cover all the relevant dimensions, we focus on three: land supply decisions, economic productivity, and the planning process.

Land Use and Supply

Although typically not the explicit focus of any research, the issue of land use and supply is implicit in many of today's most important debates. The debate about urban sprawl is at its essence a debate about whether and how the supply of undeveloped land at the urban fringe should be developed. Views vary widely. Some argue that it should not be developed at all, and the growth controls in Portland, Oregon, and Ventura County, California, are two examples of this perspective holding sway (Warner and Molotch 2001). At the other extreme, some argue that there is no imperative justifying the restriction of development of the fringe and that compact cities should not be mandated through policy and planning (Gordon and Richardson 1997, 2000).

These arguments and others highlight a central fact of land use: the specifics of the urban form depend on the decisions of individual land-owners. Although this fact is obvious to some extent, there is a relatively small literature focusing on the details and processes underlying landowners' development choices. For example, a review of economic research on government intervention and land use by Evans (1999) indicates a relatively limited set of studies on the characteristics of land supply markets, such as how they deviate from perfect competition. Similarly, Olsen (1999) notes that for housing, economic "studies of the supply of housing service are as scarce as studies of its demand are abundant" (p. 1015). Although other disciplines have been more attentive to these issues, there is clearly room for more research and a deeper understanding of this subject.

Some researchers are working to help fill this void. Molinsky (2006), for example, surveys over 2,000 owners of land at the urban fringe of four U.S. metropolitan areas. She finds similarities among owners, such as the importance of legacy and investment motives, but also differences based on varying local norms and prevailing mores.

Land Use and Economic Activity

It has long been recognized that the organization of land, particularly its use, is central to economic productivity. Basic urban economic theory highlights the importance of how land is spatially distributed in terms of where people live and work. Early models pointed to a mono-centric city in which production occurred in an urban core and workers lived in surrounding residential areas (Muth 1969; Mills 1972). Subsequent models, with increasing levels of complexity, have suggested that polycentric cities with multiple nodes featuring more intensive economic activity surrounded by residential land uses are more reasonable to expect. Empirical evidence has provided considerable support for these models (McMillen 2001; Giuliano and Small 1991; Redfearn 2007). In both the monocentric and polycentric cases, land use is segregated such that economic activity and productivity are maximized.

Apart from these more neoclassical economic models, another

strand of economic literature emphasizes the important role that proximity can play for urban growth and productivity. This literature highlights the positive spillovers that result when economic activity is bundled into a relatively small geographic space. Jacobs (1961, 1969) provides perhaps the most well-known articulation of the mechanisms underlying these spillovers. She notes the potential for agglomeration to create both within-industry spillovers, as innovations from one firm are quickly diffused to other competitors and close associates, and across-industry spillovers, as creative visionaries find ways to apply innovations from one industry to others. A considerable amount of research has sought to demonstrate and validate these positive externalities (e.g., Henderson 1988; Krugman 1991; Porter 1990). More generally, the spillovers from these agglomeration economies allow cities and urban areas to grow faster and be more productive than would be expected in a standard neoclassical economic context. Land use patterns drive the ability of industries to agglomerate. Where land use facilitates the concentration of economic activity within and across industries, positive economic externalities can prevail.

Land Use and the Planning Process

Land use considerations have always been central for the development and implementation of planning systems. Weiss (1987) shows how the first phase of the planning movement in the United States, known as the "City Beautiful" period, and the subsequent phase that sought to regulate private lands at the urban fringe both were efforts to increase the attractiveness and value of urban spaces. Early proponents of planning recognized the critical link between land use and development and argued that successful land development was contingent upon restrictions guaranteeing that proximate parcels would feature only complementary uses. Planning would provide those guarantees. This argument proved persuasive, and municipalities in urban areas throughout the United States established regulations to control the use of private lands and the development of infrastructure to support such complementary uses.

Although initial notions of urban planning argued for a complementarity between planning and good land use, this view has evolved, and planning is no longer consistently seen as a facilitator of good land use. Logan and Molotch (1987) and others have demonstrated how landowners have used the planning process to promote their growth interests in recent times. However, we have also witnessed the emergence of planning tools that act as a barrier to growth interests and changes in land use. Consider, for example, urban growth controls. These controls support and codify the status quo by freezing or severely limiting the ability of landowners to use their land in new ways (Fischel 1989).

Thus, given the competing possibilities for how planning and land use now interact, the planning process is something that needs to be managed and negotiated in order for landowners to achieve their land use objectives. As shown in Warner and Molotch's study (2001) and many others, success in this pursuit is not guaranteed and depends on the interaction of many factors.

The Interplay of Supply, Economics, and Planning in Land Use

Although they have been discussed to this point as separate considerations, planning, economics, and land supply in practice intersect and interact to determine how urban areas function. Planning affects both supply and economics. Planning rules and regulations limit landowners' choices regarding how to use their land and whether to make such land available for development. Zoning codes and growth controls are but two examples of this. Similarly, planning can dictate the economic activities that can be pursued and the potential for agglomeration forces to take hold. Enterprise zone policies represent an example of this type of planning. Both effects have direct implications for local and sometimes regional economic performance.

Economic success influences both planning and supply. Significant economic success and growth can either stymie or catalyze impulses to impose greater planning restrictions and controls on the use of undeveloped fringe land and sometimes even on the use of already-developed land closer to the urban core. Economic success can also induce landowners to consider and reconsider whether to make their lands available for development in synergistic ways that capitalize on those successes.

Finally, land supply issues are important for both planning and economics. Realities about the available land supply, including ownership patterns, topography, and access to existing infrastructure and amenities, shape conceptions of reasonable planning tenets. In addition, the character of supply, such as whether ownership is concentrated among a small number of interests, can determine the extent to which some development undertakings meet prevailing economic performance thresholds.

In short, the complexities of land use are significant, and its study presents researchers with clear challenges.

Large Landowners as a Prism for Studying These Forces and Their Interaction

Large landowners are central to all these areas. Clearly, their status of owning large tracts of land makes them important in the context of land supply. In addition, large landowners have played a critical role in the modern history of planning from its origins. Weiss (1987) shows that large landowners were quite important for the early stages of planning in the United States. They were the principal drivers of the City Beautiful movement that marked the beginning of American urban planning, and they have continued to be influential in shaping the form and scope of planning both in the United States and across the world. Finally, as owners and operators of manufacturing factories and plants, large lucrative agricultural tracts, hospitals, universities, and other enterprises, large landowners can often act as the locus of economic activity for a neighborhood, a city, or even a region.

Large landowners are also highly sensitive to these forces and their interaction. Because they often have larger-scale interests in land use outcomes, large landowners are likely to pay considerable attention to the rules governing local planning processes. In addition, because they have more resources, they are likely to be more able and willing to engage this process and try to influence it to their advantage. Broad economic forces are particularly relevant for large landowners in that they help determine the success or failure of ongoing interests. Moreover, these forces will guide the future development and land use strategies of savvy large landowners, who may seek to ride the wave of local economic trends to position or reposition their property and maximize value and profits. There is also the potential for positive feedback from large landowners in that they can be a node or attractive pole of economic activity that produces agglomerative forces resulting in growing and successful cities and regions.

An appealing aspect of large landowners is that they vary in the extent to which they choose to engage along any of these dimensions, which offers opportunities for researchers seeking to better understand land use dynamics. For example, one large landowner might view planning rules as set and immutable, whereas another might see them as malleable and potentially manipulable. Comparing and contrasting the operating and development choices and subsequent experiences of these two large landowners can shed light on how the planning process affects land supply, land use, and economic outcomes.

One might also observe two large landowners seeking to engage the planning process to further their private goals. Depending on local dynamics, there could be significant variation in the extent to which such efforts spark interest and engagement from public, nonprofit, and other private sector players. Characterizing the differences in the institutional environments that determine the nature of supplemental engagement would allow one to assess how effectively these players are able to manage the intersection of land supply, economics, and planning. Given that effective management of the process is often a critical determinant of a project's success or failure, this issue is of primary importance.

Clean, natural experiments are relatively rare. However, large landowners are sufficiently numerous and homogeneous along key dimensions, yet simultaneously varied in terms of their operating contexts, that researchers can potentially identify many tests approaching this clean standard. Well-chosen case studies of large landowners can provide myriad possibilities in terms of leveraging institutional similarity coupled with contextual variation to hone in on particular levers or issues in order to gain clear insights. Ultimately, through the results of studies such as these, one could conceivably develop an overarching framework to guide thinking about land use issues.

It is this recognition that serves as the foundation for the text. We divide the chapters into three parts that highlight how large landowners influence and shape land use in terms of supply, economic development, and planning. The cases within each section have been chosen to highlight the breadth of potential research rather than examples of the natural experiments just discussed. In this regard, we include two studies that examine large landowners in non-U.S. contexts. These international studies emphasize the generality of the land use issues being studied.

The first part focuses on how land supply is influenced by the interests and decisions of large landowners. The initial chapter confronts the ongoing evolution of the urban fringe in the United States and the associated debates regarding land use and the promotion of economic growth, sprawl, urban growth controls, and individual property rights. In "Understanding Large Landholders on the Urban Fringe: A Supply-Side Perspective," Pengyu Zhu and Raphael W. Bostic examine these issues by analyzing the backgrounds and experiences of large landowners at the urban fringe, as well as their perspectives on the relationship between the development of fringe lands and quality of life.

The data that Zhu and Bostic use are drawn from a 2002 Lincoln Institute of Land Policy survey of owners of parcels at the urban fringe in four U.S. metropolitan areas that vary in terms of geographic location and history. The authors examine only the responses of those landowners who control parcels larger than 15 acres; these landowners represent about 40 percent of the overall respondent sample.

The results suggest that large fringe landowners are as ambivalent about urban growth and development of fringe lands as the broader population. The proportion of respondents in each area who believed that the development of the fringe was beneficial or detrimental to quality of life approximates observed proportions in the respective populations. In short, large fringe landowners seem to mirror the conflicted view of the general population regarding development on the fringe. This suggests that future development on the fringe will continue to occur in fits and starts as individual large landowners make their own, somewhat idiosyncratic decisions about whether and how to develop their lands. The authors identify several areas where large fringe landowners differ from smaller ones, the most significant being their greater propensity to be business-oriented and to face development pressure. However, this does not appear to translate into a greater propensity to sell or transfer their land. Although many findings were consistent across the fringes of these four metropolitan areas, the analysis also revealed some significant differences across the metropolitan areas, suggesting an important role for culture, local attitudes, and place-based land use regulations.

Land supply issues, particularly on the fringe of metropolitan areas, are not limited to an American context or to developed nations with long histories of urbanization. They are also relevant in developing countries that are beginning to more intensively engage the developed world economically and that consequently are facing the same pressures to convert land from rural uses to more productive residential and commercial applications. Cosmas Uchenna Ikejiofor's "Customary Landholders and the Planning Process in Contemporary Enugu, Nigeria" documents land supply issues arising as a result of the rapid urbanization of one metropolitan area that is strongly affected by global economic forces.

Ikejiofor begins by describing the institutional context in Enugu, a region in southeastern Nigeria, which differs considerably from that in many industrialized nations. Indigenous customary landowners linked by communal and familial affiliations control the bulk of land at the periphery, and family landholding is the dominant form of ownership and control. The individual communal and family entities in Enugu are thus analogous to the large landowners surveyed in chapter 1. Ikejiofor conducts a survey of the Enugu landowners to assess how they are responding to their needs as their family situations evolve and to increasing pressure from speculators seeking to acquire the land for urban development.

The survey's results indicate that most decisions to sell were driven by urgent family needs rather than by a more objective profit motive, and that despite the distress sellers found themselves in, their behavior was strategic in the sense that they rarely sold all their holdings and often sold parcels that allowed them to preserve their lifestyle to a degree. Ikejiofor's work also highlights the importance of institutions. He documents that the sale of customary landholdings represents a broader transition in Nigerian land ownership from customary land rights, which are perceived as less secure, to more formal title control.

The second part of the volume focuses on the role of large landowners as local economic catalysts. In their chapter, "The Neighborhood Dynamics of Hospitals as Large Landowners," Bostic, LaVonna B. Lewis, and David C. Sloane evaluate hospitals' influence on the spatial pattern of economic activity in a neighborhood. Prior research has found that hospitals are important in spurring economic activity at the neighborhood level. Bostic, Lewis, and Sloane focus on two key unanswered questions: (1) whether the extent to which hospitals act as a catalyst for local economic activity varies with the characteristics of the local area; and (2) whether the extent of a hospital's influence varies with characteristics of the hospital. The authors use one dimension—size—in analyzing this second question.

Their analysis relies on data from a survey of parcels located within a one-mile radius of seven Los Angeles hospitals that vary by geography, size, and neighborhood location. The census allows the authors to characterize the land use around the hospital as either residential or commercial and, within the commercial sector, as either health-related or not. Intensity of commercial land uses, particularly health-related uses, is used as the metric for establishing the extent of a hospital's economic drawing power.

As in previous research studies, the authors find clear evidence that hospitals act as an economic catalyst: commercial and health-related land uses become more intense as one nears the hospital. Thus, hospitals appear to be attractive nodes that promote within-industry linkages and the potential for positive agglomeration economies. Overall, two distinct patterns for this commercial activity—corridors and clusters—were observed. Despite the general result, the authors also find that the extent to which this is true appears to vary with neighborhood characteristics. Neighborhood income plays a role, as does race, and the interactions are complex, sometimes conforming to expectations and sometimes not.

The second chapter in the economics section is a case study of the economic role played by a university, which is one class of large landholder that has received some academic attention (Perry and Weiwel 2005; Wiewel and Knapp 2005). John C. Brown and Jacqueline Geoghegan expand and augment this literature with their chapter, "Bringing the Campus to the Community: An Examination of the Clark University Park Partnership After Ten Years." This study evaluates the economic impact of a large landholder, Clark University, which has taken a more active role in economic development than did the hospitals studied by Bostic, Lewis, and Sloane.

Brown and Geoghegan detail how Clark University, located in a declining community in Worcester, Massachusetts, worked to reverse the decline and promote neighborhood stability, development, and growth. The main vehicle for Clark was a campus-community partnership known as the University Park Partnership (UPP), which grew out of a collaboration with a local community development corporation. The UPP sought both to improve the physical look of the community and to create neighborhood amenities and opportunities for local residents.

The authors assess whether the new menu of neighborhood amenities has translated into measurable economic benefit. Assuming that all neighborhood amenities should be capitalized into the prices of the local properties, they measure benefit by using property values. Brown and Geoghegan use two empirical approaches. The first relies on local repeat sales indexes to compare house price appreciation in the UPP neighborhood, the city of Worcester, and the broader metropolitan area. The second method involves estimating a hedonic regression that distinguishes values for properties within and just outside the eligibility boundary for UPP neighborhood amenities.

The results using both methods indicate that there has been a strong capitalization effect associated with the UPP, particularly in the years marked by a strong housing market recovery throughout New England. The findings suggest that the activities of Clark successfully catalyzed neighborhood change and, at least by one measure, helped turn around the Main Street neighborhood.

The final part examines how large landowners have engaged the planning process and includes two studies focusing on landowners in very different contexts from those in the previous chapters. "Large Landowners as Plan Makers: St. Joe and the Future of the Florida Panhandle," by Timothy S. Chapin, examines the evolution of the St. Joe Company from a timber and paper company into the major land developer in the panhandle region of Florida. St. Joe represents a major class of large landowners—companies that have relied on the agricultural bounty of undeveloped hinterlands to produce goods that are no longer economical to produce—that have emerged as important players in the land use disposition process and are likely to become more salient in the years to come.

The St. Joe case is particularly interesting because the rise of St. Joe as a development company has coincided with an ever-evolving planning process in Florida. Chapin was thus able to observe St. Joe being affected by as well as influencing the rules established by the state's planning process. Chapin tracks several St. Joe development proposals in Florida's Franklin and Bay counties, where St. Joe has taken a lead role in the formation of comprehensive planning visions for the region.

Chapin's study reveals that large landowners provide both opportunities and challenges for the planning process. On the opportunity side, the interests of large landowners make them amenable to the private provision of public facilities and public open space and can lead to improved planning processes at the state and local levels. In terms of challenges, large landowners are likely to co-opt the planning process or serve as a lightning rod for community disapproval. Chapin notes that these challenges are to some degree not unique to large landowners, but rather may arise for any large-scale development project.

The closing chapter returns to an international context and examines large landowners of the public sector. In "Public Sector Land Developers in New Delhi and Bangalore, India: A Comparison of Processes and Outcomes," David L. Gladstone and Kameswara Sreenivas Kolapalli conduct a comparative study of powerful public agencies in two of India's fastest-growing metropolitan areas. Like all large landowners, these agencies engage land use along multiple dimensions. Where they differ from the other large landowners analyzed in this volume is that they often have explicit authority as the planning rule-makers and therefore set the rules that define the context in which they operate.

The authors use indirect methods to evaluate how the different mandates given the Delhi Development Authority (DDA) and Bangalore's Karnataka Industrial Areas Development Board (KIADB) and the different approaches taken by the agencies have influenced land use and development patterns in the two cities. The authors hypothesize that the KIADB's explicit focus on investment promotion and economic development for industrial uses, in contrast to the broader focus of the DDA and its more socially oriented goals, should result in very different land use patterns and different infrastructure investment, and would help ease social problems.

Although the authors observe quite similar overall conditions in both cities—high land prices, acute pressure to develop, and overwhelmed infrastructure—they also note important differences between the two cities and attribute these differences to the different roles the agencies play as landowners, planners, and developers. In particular, the DDA's broader mandate and planning engagement has meant that the affordable-housing, infrastructure, and jobs-housing balance problems are less acute in Delhi. The authors also note that each city features multiple land markets: one for more affluent families, one for speculators focused on the fringe, and one for those families using unauthorized housing. However, the reasons behind the emergence of these multiple markets differ for Delhi and Bangalore. The authors argue that in Delhi DDA limits on private-sector land development (a planning function), which could ease pressures at the fringe, have sparked considerable speculation just beyond the DDA's jurisdictional authority. In Bangalore the tremendous power of the information technology industry is the source of the speculative energy.

The chapters in this volume, in addition to highlighting issues in each subject area, indicate the value in shedding light on large landowners. The studies individually offer new and interesting insights into central issues associated with land use and development. Taken together, they offer potentially even more. The volume's chapters span a rich cross-section of large landowners in terms of industry, geography, and development context. Other cases exist, and considering the variation in circumstances and outcomes across these cases, as well as those in this volume, should be highly useful for obtaining a clearer and deeper understanding of how land use, land supply, planning, industrial structure, and economics interact to shape outcomes. We are hopeful that this volume serves as a catalyst for researchers to consider the study of large landowners in the pursuit of such clarity and that it leads to the development of new frameworks for characterizing these interesting and complex arrangements.

I

LAND SUPPLY DECISIONS

1

UNDERSTANDING LARGE LANDHOLDERS ON THE URBAN FRINGE

A Supply-Side Perspective

Pengyu Zhu and Raphael W. Bostic

Globalization, decentralization, and technological innovation continue to have a profound impact on cities. Cities exist in a competitive marketplace and must promote economic growth. A major focus of the literature on urban development, such "economic logic" suggests that cities should conceive of themselves as efficiency-maximizing entities and hold a unitary interest in enhancing economic productivity (Savitch and Kantor 2002). Under this economic logic, cities are quickly growing, in terms of both population and geographic area. Spatial expansion has put pressures on land at the fringe of these developed areas. How the supply of this fringe land is managed and operated as a transition between urban and undeveloped areas is important for both types of areas.

Because land ownership is often distributed among many interests, the management of fringe lands depends on the collective decisions of various agents. These decisions, in turn, depend on the characteristics, behaviors, interests, and intentions of the landowners. How land owners make decisions of whether and how to supply fringe land for development is important because urban growth will be determined by the extent to which these fringe lands are successfully incorporated into the urban fabric. If landowners actively engage, urban areas can continue to grow and urbanize. But growth brings with it changes in lifestyle that have benefits as well as costs. Fearing the costs associated with growth, owners might prefer the status quo, and this can establish competing motives for land disposition.

In this chapter we examine these issues by analyzing the perspective of fringe landowners in order to better understand their impact on land supply. We use data collected in a 2002–2003 telephone survey sponsored by the Lincoln Institute of Land Policy and the Joint Center for Housing Studies at Harvard University of owners of undeveloped fringe land in Sacramento, California; Charlotte, North Carolina; Portland, Oregon; and Austin, Texas. The survey sought information on the characteristics, behaviors, interests, and intentions of these fringe landowners, and especially their decisions related to land use and the subdivision, development, sale, and transfer of their parcels. For details on the criteria for region selection, sampling methodology, and survey implementation, see Molinsky (2006).

Molinsky's study (2006) evaluated landowners of fringe lands of five acres or larger. Our study is a more focused analysis, examining only the survey's 837 large fringe landowners—defined, for the purposes of this study, as owners holding 15 acres or more—because decisions about larger parcels have a greater impact on both economic performance and quality of life. The behavior of large landowners directly affects the stability and health of the land market. An interesting question is whether the class of large fringe landowners differs in important ways from the group of smaller owners along the urban fringe.

The survey also allows us to assess the extent to which large fringe landowner views differ across geography. The four metropolitan areas in the survey have distinct and differentiated histories and prevailing cultures. The analysis therefore can speak to whether and how history and culture affect land supply decisions.

Survey Results

The data provide a clear picture about who owns fringe lands, how these owners are currently using their land, and how they participate in the land market. The following sections describe the owners' characteristics, the characteristics of the land, and the owners' behaviors, as well as regional differences among the four metropolitan areas (also metropolitan statistical areas, or MSAs).

Owners' Characteristics

In all four regions, the vast majority of large landowners possessed their land through individual ownership or family ownership (see table 1.1). Significantly smaller numbers of owners in Portland and Sacramento possessed their land through partnerships or family-held corporations. Other types of ownership were rare. This pattern confirms that, at least in our study regions, the supply of land for future housing market and urban growth is in the hands of many large landholders, who will make decisions about when to sell, subdivide, and develop their fringe land. It also raises the possibility that large fringe land disposition will be more complex because individuals and families are more likely to have multiple motives than corporate landowners, who are typically expected to consider only economic benefits and capital gains. We explore these individual multiple motivations in more detail in ensuing sections.

Table 1.2 reports the demographic characteristics of large fringe landowners. The average age of surveyed landowners was 61, and respondents were mostly male and white—the large fringe landowners represented a less diverse pool than the general population. According to the 2006 census, the percentage of whites in the central cities of Austin, Charlotte, Portland, and Sacramento was only 59.1, 54.7, 78.1, and 50.5 percent, respectively.

The large fringe landowners in the survey were well educated, and college-degree attainment among this group exceeded prevailing metropolitan area levels. For example, 56 percent of landowners in the Austin area reported holding a bachelor's degree or higher, whereas

Table 1.1 Legal form of parcel ownership (percentage)

Form of ownership	Austin	Charlotte	Portland	Sacramento	Total
Individual or family	92.5	91.2	74.5	74.5	82.3
Partnership	3.1	3.7	6.0	11.5	6.0
Family-held corporation	2.7	1.9	12.1	7.3	5.4
Other corporation	0.4	1.9	4.7	5.5	2.9
All other forms	1.2	1.4	2.7	8.3	3.4
N	255	215	149	218	837

Table 1.2 Landowner characteristics in four central cities

	Austin	Charlotte	Portland	Sacramento	Total
Year of birth					
Median	1943	1942	1941	1942	1942
Mean	1942	1942	1941	1942	1942
Standard deviation	13	12	12.7	14.8	13.2
Minimum	1910	1916	1918	1907	1907
Maximum	1977	1972	1972	1981	1981
N	247	206	143	211	807
Gender (percentage)					
Male	60.9	58.8	51.4	56.0	57.3
Female	39.1	41.2	48.6	44.0	42.7
N	253	211	148	218	830
Race (percentage)					
White	91.67	94.2	93.71	81.9	90.15
Black	1.98	1.45	0	0	0.99
Hispanic	3.57	0	0	0	1.11
Asian/Pacific Islander	0	0	0.7	3.33	0.99
Native American	0	0.48	0	0.95	0.37
Other/don't know/refused	2.77	3.87	5.6	13.81	6.4
N	252	207	143	210	812
Education (percentage attained)					
High school or less	19.05	37.68	32.17	27.14	28.2
Some college	21.03	21.74	21.68	26.19	22.66
College graduate	31.75	23.67	27.97	30	28.57
Postgraduate	24.21	14.98	16.78	12.86	17.61
Don't know/refused	3.96	1.93	1.4	3.81	2.96
N	252	207	143	210	812
Primary profession (percentage)					
Farmer, rancher, forester	12.20	9.95	27.52	32.57	19.71
Real estate invest./devel.	5.12	4.74	4.03	6.88	5.29
Other employment	45.28	39.34	34.23	25.69	36.66
Retired	36.61	45.50	32.89	33.03	37.26
Don't know/refused	0.79	0.47	1.34	1.83	1.08
N	254	211	149	218	832

Note: Primary professions are defined as the mode of employment to which the landowners devoted more than 50 percent of their time.

the 2006 census reported a 42.9 percent rate for the greater Austin area. Smaller disparities were observed in the other metropolitan areas.

Interestingly, only 19.7 percent of the large fringe landowner respondents reported agriculture—farming, ranching, or forestry—as their primary profession. However, variations across these four regions are significant, with low percentages in Austin and Charlotte (12.2 and 10.0 percent, respectively) and relatively high percentages in Portland and Sacramento (27.5 and 32.6 percent, respectively). The higher rates in Portland and Sacramento may be due to particular local features. The stringent growth-control regulations in Portland may allow agricultural uses to persist more there, and Sacramento has historically had a strong agricultural presence because of its suitable soil and weather. Across the board, few large fringe landowners considered themselves real estate development or investment professionals.

Although most large fringe landowners reported high incomes (greater than $50,000), nearly one-quarter reported incomes below

Table 1.3   Distribution of owners by income and net worth

	Austin	Charlotte	Portland	Sacramento	Total
Reported income (percentage)					
Less than $10,000	2.8	1.4	1.4	0.0*	1.5
$10,000 to $19,999	2.4	1.9	2.8	1.0†	2.0
$20,000 to $29,999	4.8	3.9	5.6	2.9*	4.2
$30,000 to $39,999	5.6	10.1	7.0	5.2†	6.9
$40,000 to $49,999	8.7	15.5	12.6	7.6†	10.8
$50,000 to $74,999	9.9	16.9	16.1	15.2	14.2
$75,000 to $99,999	15.1	11.6	12.6	12.4	13.1
$100,000 to $124,999	6.0	4.8	8.4	7.1	6.4
$125,000 or more	19.0	9.7	13.3	22.4*	16.5
Don't know/refused	25.8	24.2	20.3	26.2	24.5
N	252	207	143	210	812
Average monthly debt/income (percentage)	26.2	17.2	17.7	19.6	20.5
N	173	154	116	151	594
Reported net worth (percentage)					
Less than $500,000	30.16	25.12	16.8*	13.3*	22.2
$500,000 to $999,999	21.03	23.67	26.57	19.05*	22.17
$1,000,000 to $4,999,999	15.08	15.94	23.08	30.48*	20.69
$5,000,000 or more	3.97	3.86	9.09†	9.05†	6.16
Don't know/refused	29.76	31.4	24.48	28.09	28.82
N	252	207	143	210	812
Average land holdings/net worth (percentage)	49.4	59.6	63.6	65.4	58.9
N	184	148	125	165	622

Note: For average monthly income as a percentage of debt, debt includes mortgage, auto, personal, and farm loans as well as revolving credit card debt.

* Significantly different from all other regions at $p < 0.05$.

† Significantly different from two regions at $p < 0.05$. This notation is consistent across all tables in this chapter.

$50,000 (see table 1.3). This might suggest that income is an important consideration for at least a significant minority of the survey respondents. We note significant regional variation here, with a low percentage in Sacramento (16.7 percent) and a high rate in Portland (29.4 percent) and Charlotte (32.8 percent). We see similar disparities with respect to net worth: Sacramento large fringe landowners were much less likely than those in other cities to have a net worth less than $1 million. Overall, Austin and Charlotte had very similar wealth distributions at all levels.

For all these large fringe landowners, land was a significant component of their wealth. Overall, nearly 60 percent of their total worth consisted of the fringe landholding. Moreover, as in Molinsky's study (2006), we see that owners involved in agriculture had the highest percentage of their wealth in land.

Land Characteristics

PARCEL SIZES

The lower bound for consideration in this study was 15 acres, but the typical respondent owned much more land (see table 1.4). The mean and median holdings were about 70 and 37 acres, respectively. Interestingly, we find a significant relationship between parcel acreage and owners' age and retirement status, suggesting that older and retired landowners tend to have larger parcels. The sample-wide averages mask variation across the four MSAs. Landholdings in Austin and Sacramento were much larger than those in Charlotte and Portland. Also, we observe a negative correlation between parcel size and perceived intensity of development pressure. This might reflect the fact that larger parcels can, if developed, lead to considerable changes in land use. Thus, developers pursue them most aggressively.

CURRENT LAND USE

Nearly all the land in the survey (81.7 percent) was devoted to agricultural use, and agricultural use was the most common use found on at least some portion of these large fringe land parcels (see table 1.5). Moreover, where a single land use prevailed (when at least 90 percent of the land was devoted to a single use), that use was most often agricultural. Charlotte lagged a bit in this regard, but even there agricultural use far outstripped secondary uses. In all four MSAs, residential and open space uses were distant second considerations. In addition,

Table 1.4   Parcel sizes in four central cities

	Austin	Charlotte	Portland	Sacramento	Total
Parcel size (acres)					
Mean	99.7	42.5	45.3	80.4	70.3
Median	52.9	30.0	28.0	38.5	37.0
Maximum	1237.2	237.5	405.0	657.0	1237.2
Minimum	15.0	15.0	15.0	15.0	15.0
N	255	215	149	218	837
Mean parcel size by development pressure (acres)					
Intense pressure	99.3	38.6	29.7	47.3	61.8
Moderate pressure	105.6	47.1	42.1	73.6	70.3
Weak pressure	95.1	42.0	51.9	88.0	73.9
N	255	215	149	218	837

28.7 percent of landowners reported that their land was used for recreation in addition to other uses; a significantly higher percentage of Austin large fringe landowners reported this use compared with landowners in the other areas.[1]

CONDITIONS AT THE TIME OF LAND ACQUISITION

Because conditions and circumstances can change considerably over time, the survey sought to distinguish current uses and motives from uses and motives at the time of acquisition. To that end, the survey asked landowners a series of questions about when, how, and for what intended purposes they acquired their fringe land.

The responses suggest that this additional focus was warranted, as the large fringe landowners on average owned their parcels for over 20 years (see table 1.6). Austin large fringe landowners were newer than those in other MSAs, but even these owners can be considered long-term holders of their properties using objective standards. Figure 1.1 illustrates the distribution of parcels by year of acquisition for the four regions.[2] The sample includes a mix of longtime landowners and recent owners. Overall, 44 percent of these large fringe lands were ac-

---

1. Since recreational use frequently overlaps with other uses, the survey simply asked whether the land was used for recreation and did not ask for the percentage of land in recreational use.

2. For land acquired through multiple transactions (purchase, inheritance, gift, etc.), we used the year of the first transaction as the year of acquisition. We also excluded those who answered "don't know" or refused to answer from our calculation.

Table 1.5 Land uses in four central cities

	Austin	Charlotte	Portland	Sacramento	Total
Land uses by parcel (percentage)					
Any agricultural	79.6	68.8	87.9	79.4	78.3
Any open/idle use	24.7	47.9	34.2	22.0	31.7
Any commercial/industrial	3.5	4.2	7.4	5.0	4.8
Any nonfarm residential	29.8	31.2	17.4	27.1	27.2
Any other	2.7	1.9	3.4	2.3	2.5
Major land use by parcel					
Agricultural	63.9	40.0*	58.4	63.8	56.8
Undeveloped (open/idle)	15.3	19.1*	7.4	11.0	13.7
Commercial/industrial	1.2	0.5	1.3	1.8	1.2
Uses of land captured in survey (percent)					
Agricultural	87.2	62.4*	81.4	83.8	81.7
Open/idle	8.4	28.9*	13.5	10.1	12.7
Commercial/industrial	1.1	1.2	2.9	2.7	1.8
Nonfarm residential	2.6	7.1*	1.7	3.1	3.3
Other	0.7	0.3	0.5	0.2	0.5
Recreational use	42.4*	29.8	20.1	17.4	28.7
N	255	215	149	218	837

Note: A use is considered "major" if 90 percent of the land is devoted to that use. Other land uses include utility, transportation, and institutional uses. Because recreational use frequently overlaps with other uses, the survey asked only if the land was used for recreation and did not ask the percentage of land in recreational use.

* Significantly different from all other regions at $p < 0.05$.

quired before 1980. Landowners who acquired their land in the 1980s and 1990s account for 52.4 percent. Only 3.6 percent of landowners acquired their land after 2000. An important side note: the long-term landowners tended to amass their holdings through multiple transactions.

Purchase and inheritance were the dominant means of acquisition for large fringe landowners. Together, these methods explain how more than 90 percent of the survey respondents gained their parcels. Proportions across the four MSAs are similar with the exception of Charlotte, where significantly more landowners inherited their land (41.1 percent) or received their land as a gift (3.7 percent). We find a consistently significant correlation between parcel size and inheritance of land in all regions—inheritors tend to have larger parcels than buyers.

Among purchasers, responses indicate multiple important criteria in deciding to buy. Overall, the three most important features influenc-

Table 1.6   Statistics on acquisition of land and decision factors

	Austin	Charlotte	Portland	Sacramento	Total
Year of land acquisition					
Mean	1985	1981	1978	1978	1981
Median	1987	1985	1980	1981	1984
N	236	195	145	204	780
Acquisition method (percentage)					
Bought parcel	68.2	48.1*	71.8	73.7	65.2
Inherited parcel	25.5	41.1*	25.5	19.8	28.0
Received parcel as gift	2.0	3.7*	2.7	2.3	2.6
Multiple methods	4.3	7.0*	0.0	4.2	4.2
N	255	214	149	217	835
Percentage reporting factor to be important for purchase decision					
Proximity to municipal services	10.9	7.8	8.4	13.8*	10.7
Commute time to job	14.9	16.5	16.8	22.5*	17.8
Amenities and services	28.7	23.3	28.0	21.9	25.6
Suitability for agriculture or ranching	37.9	28.2	43.9	58.1*	43.2
Price or terms of sale	44.3	37.9	38.3	44.4	41.9
Property taxes	14.9	14.6	14.0	11.9	13.8
Suitability for family	32.8	38.8	38.3	37.5	36.4
Proximity to family or friends	12.1	24.3	0.0*	21.3	14.7
N	174	103	107	160	544

Note: For land acquired through multiple transactions, we used the year of the first transaction as the year of acquisition. Statistics on the year of acquisition exclude those who answered "don't know/refused." Importance is rated on a scale of 1 to 5. Percentages indicate those who rated the factor a 5 (very important).

* Significantly different from all other regions at $p < 0.05$.

ing owners' decisions were suitability for agriculture or ranching, price or terms of sale, and suitability for family. Nearby amenities and services, such as scenery, open space, and schools, were also cited as important features. Other features, such as proximity to municipal services or family and friends, tended to be less important to a landowner's purchase decision. These patterns were consistent across all regions with only minor exceptions.

Perhaps not surprisingly given current motivations and uses, at the time of acquisition a solid majority (75.4 percent) of landowners intended to use their undeveloped fringe land for agriculture, with or without other uses (see table 1.7). Many landowners intended to accommodate other uses as well: residential, recreational, and open space uses were commonly intended additional uses.

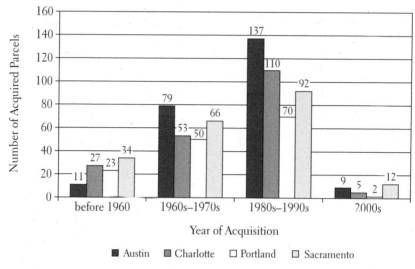

Figure 1.1 Year of land acquisition for four regions.

About 27.8 percent of respondents reported an interest at the time they acquired the property in taking steps to transition at least some of their land to more public uses through either subdivision or development. Roughly similar percentages of landowners intended to subdivide and develop their land, though owners in Sacramento were more likely to develop their land in the future than subdivide their parcels. Most large fringe landowners had long-term horizons, reflected in their expectation of holding their properties for 10 years or longer. This strongly suggests that the large fringe landowners in our sample are not speculators hoping for a quick return by flipping properties. Rather, they appear to be more complex agents seeking more than simple returns.

A comparison of current uses with intended uses at the time of acquisition reveals that the percentage of parcels with any agricultural use has remained very stable over time. The percentage of parcels with some undeveloped land did not change too much either, except in Portland, where this percentage almost doubled (from 18.1 to 34.2 percent) compared with landowners' original intentions. Perhaps this is due to Portland's rigorous land use regulations and various growth-control policies. Interestingly, the percentage of parcels with any nonfarm residential use declined in Austin, Charlotte, and Port-

Table 1.7   Intentions for property at time of acquisition

	Austin	Charlotte	Portland	Sacramento	Total
Owner intentions at acquisition (percentage)					
Agricultural	74.1	66.0	87.2	78.0	75.4
Open/idle	29.8	40.5	18.1	18.8	27.6
Rural commercial/industrial	11.4	12.6	18.8	14.2	13.7
Urban or suburban commercial/industrial	3.9	7.9	5.4	7.3	6.1
Nonfarm residential	37.6	45.1	26.8	28.0	35.1
Recreational use	32.5	22.3	14.8	14.2	22.0
N	255	215	149	218	837
Other intentions at acquisition (percentage)					
Future subdivision	12.2	19.1	26.2	16.5	17.6
Future development	18.8	18.1	27.5	28.0	22.6
Hold land for					
10 or more years	85.9	89.3	91.9	87.2	88.2
6 to 10 years	7.5	3.7	4.7	5.5	5.5
5 years or less	4.3	2.8	2.0	6.0	3.9
Don't know	2.4	4.2	1.3	1.4	2.4
Enlarge parcel through acquisition "very important"	13.7	15.8	14.1	14.7	14.6
Lease land as farm/ranch	28.2	20.9	22.1	22.9	23.9
N	255	215	149	218	837

Note: The questionnaire allowed for multiple intended uses at the time of acquisition.

land, whereas it remained stable in Sacramento. The percentage of parcels with current commercial or industrial uses was significantly and consistently smaller than the percentage of landowners who originally intended to use their land for commercial or industrial purposes. This is consistent with the view that fringe landowners either overestimated the pace of urban growth in their regions or underestimated the power of planning and land use controls. The percentage of parcels with any recreational use (either public or private) also slightly increased in all four regions.

Owner Behaviors

PREVIOUS PARTICIPATION IN THE LAND MARKET

Landowners were asked directly if they had ever entered the land market through the sale or donation of an adjacent parcel (see table 1.8). Only a small portion of them had done so: the figures ranged from

Table 1.8   Previous sales and transfers of adjacent parcels

	Austin	Charlotte	Portland	Sacramento	Total
Percentage selling or transferring adjacent parcel	13.3	23.3*	12.1	15.6	16.2
N	255	215	149	218	837
If sold, year of sale of transfer					
Mean	1992	1988	1982	1984	1987
Median	1996	1992	1982	1989	1990
N	33	43	17	28	121
Reason for sale or transfer (percentage)					
Transfer to relative	26.5	42.0*	16.7	26.5	30.9
Nonfinancial family or life-cycle issues	5.9	0.0	5.6	2.9	2.9
Assist neighbor/friend	8.8	14.0*	5.6	5.9	9.6
Received good offer	14.7	20.0*	5.6	8.8	14.0
Needed money	26.5*	6.0*	11.1	11.8	13.2
Protect land from development	0.0	0.0	0.0	0.0	0.0
Tax advantages	0.0	4.0	0.0	5.9	2.9
Better investment elsewhere	0.0	2.0	5.6	0.0	1.5
Development pressures	2.9	2.0	0.0	2.9	2.2
Other	17.6	14.0	61.1	35.3	26.5
N	34	50	18	34	136

Note: Multiple reasons for the sale or transfer were permitted. Nonfinancial issues included retirement, divorce, a new job, and the desire for a change of pace.

* Significantly different from all other regions at $p < 0.05$.

12.1 percent in Portland to 23.3 percent in Charlotte, with an average of 16.2 percent across all four regions. These landowners were more likely to own larger properties or to have owned their property for a relatively long time. In terms of the timing of sales and transfers, significant regional differences existed. Portland had the earliest mean and median year of sale or transfer (both at 1982), whereas Austin landowners reported significantly more recent transactions, with a mean year of 1992 and median year of 1996. This is consistent with the fact that land pressures due to rapid growth have become acute in Austin relatively recently compared with the other MSAs.

Among those who had sold or transferred adjacent land, the most common reason for the transaction was to transfer land to children or other family members; the need for money, a strong offer, and assisting a neighbor or friend were secondary motives. Significantly, none mentioned using the sale or transfer to protect adjacent land from development. There were also slight variations across regions. The need for money led significantly more landowners in Austin to sell or transfer their land, whereas a significantly higher percentage of landowners in Charlotte were motivated by a desire to transfer land to children or other family members. For Charlotte large fringe landowners, reasons such as assisting a neighbor or friend and receiving a good offer were also significantly more common than in other regions, whereas the need for money was significantly less common.

Whether or not they had sold or transferred land previously, a large percentage of landowners had received offers from interested buyers (see table 1.9). In the year preceding the survey, 39.4 percent of landowners were approached with an offer to purchase some of or all their property; the percentages in Charlotte and Sacramento were significantly higher than in Austin and Portland. A slightly smaller percentage of landowners stated that they had received offers from people wishing to develop their land; the percentages in Charlotte and Sacramento once again were significantly higher than in Austin and Portland.

CURRENT PARTICIPATION IN LAND MARKET

Landowners who plan to sell or transfer their land will be directly involved in the parcelization of fringe land and the change in land supply. At the time of the survey, 27.2 percent of these large fringe landholders were considering selling or giving away some of or all their property; there was no significant difference across the four regions (see table 1.10). When asked to rate the various factors affecting their current land sale and transfer considerations, over half the landowners in each region ranked receiving a good offer as "very important."

Table 1.9   Previous offers from interested buyers

	Austin	Charlotte	Portland	Sacramento	Total
Percentage receiving offers					
To purchase in the past year	32.2	45.6	34.2	45.4	39.4
To develop in the past year	25.9	43.7	30.9	43.1	35.8
N	255	215	149	218	837

Table 1.10 Land sales and transfers

	Austin	Charlotte	Portland	Sacramento	Total
Percentage currently interested in land sale/transfer	25.5	27.0	26.2	30.3	27.2
N	255	215	149	218	837
For those considering sale, percentage reporting factor as very important					
Good offer	55.4	53.4	59.0	50.0	53.9
Need for money	23.1	20.7	20.5	21.2	21.5
Transfer land to relatives	23.1	31.0	17.9	19.7	23.2
Nonfinancial family or life-cycle issues	10.8	19.0	10.3	16.7	14.5
Assist a neighbor or friend	6.2	3.4	0.0	4.5	3.9
Protect land from development	0.0	0.0	0.0	0.0	0.0
Tax advantages	16.9	22.4	10.3	12.1	15.8
Better investment elsewhere	12.3	22.4	12.8	19.7	17.1
Pace of development in area	0.0	0.0	0.0	0.0	0.0
N	65	58	39	66	228
For those not considering sale, percentage reporting factor as very important					
Good offer	17.4	16.6	21.8	26.3	20.2
Need for money	18.9	16.6	13.6	9.2	14.9
Transfer land to relatives	47.4	52.2	37.3	39.5	44.8
Nonfinancial family or life-cycle issues	7.9	8.9	10.9	3.3	7.6
Assist a neighbor or friend	4.7	6.4	3.6	5.3	5.1
Protect land from development	0.0	0.0	0.0	0.0	0.0
Tax advantages	13.7	15.9	16.4	9.9	13.8
Better investment elsewhere	7.9	10.2	7.3	11.2	9.2
Pace of development in area	0.0	0.0	0.0	0.0	0.0
N	190	157	110	152	609
Percentage of owners who would consider the land uses intended by the bidder in sales decision	65.5	65.6	59.4	55.9	62.0
N	235	209	138	202	784

Note: Importance is rated on a scale of 1 to 5. Percentages indicate those who rated the factor a 5 (very important). This survey question accepted multiple responses; therefore, the percentage for each factor may not sum to 100 percent. Landowners responding "don't know/refused" were excluded from the count of those landowners that would consider the intended land use of the bidder in the sale decision.

Owners gave less importance to other factors, such as money pressures, bequest motives, nonfinancial family or life-cycle issues, tax advantages, and better alternative investments. Across regions, this ranking was strikingly stable even though landowners reported significant regional differences in their previous sales or transactions.

The importance of receiving a good offer increased tremendously for large fringe landowners considering selling or transferring their land (from 14.0 percent for those who had previously sold land to 53.9 percent). Perhaps this is due to the increased recognition that emerged during the 1990s and early 2000s, as residential house prices skyrocketed, that real estate wealth is an important vehicle for building household wealth. The importance of the need for money as a factor in considering a sale also increased, from 13.2 percent to 21.5 percent, whereas the importance of transferring land to children or other family members declined. Three other factors—nonfinancial family or life-cycle issues, tax advantages, and better alternative investments—also significantly increased in their importance, moving from having only very minor influence (around 2 percent of landowners rated them as "very important") on previous land sales and transfers to playing a relatively important role (around 16 percent of landowners rated them as "very important") in current land sale and transfer considerations. The desire to assist a neighbor or friend, which was "very important" to 9.6 percent of landowners in their previous land sales and transfers, was rated the same way by only 3.9 percent of landowners in their current land sale and transfer considerations. These broad trends suggest that investment objectives and financial pressures have become more salient for this subset of large fringe landowners, whereas some familial and personal motives have declined somewhat in importance. The attention to taxes and investments also suggests an increased sophistication among large fringe landowners over time.

We noted earlier the issue of multiple motives and the complexity of the large fringe landowner population. This is clearly highlighted when one looks at landowners who were not currently considering land sales or transfers. This group, which made up nearly three-quarters of the survey sample, ranked these factors differently. In all four regions, these landowners tended to place more value on transferring land to children or other family members and less value on receiving a good offer, the need for money, and the existence of better investment opportunities elsewhere compared with those who were actually considering land sales and transfers. Nearly 50 percent of this subgroup of large fringe landowners reported the bequest motive as most important, far and away the largest consideration.

Another striking finding is that 62 percent of the large fringe landowners (across both subgroups) reported that they would take into account the bidders' intended land uses when making their land sale decisions. This percentage, which remained relatively stable across all four regions, demonstrates a clear role for quality-of-life and community considerations. Most current large fringe landowners appear to be sensitive to prior development patterns and do not want to be seen as contributing to negative development trends if they are perceived to exist. This result emphasizes the point that large fringe landowners are more complex than typical corporate landowners; fringe development and urban expansion will therefore be more nuanced than one might initially expect.

FUTURE PLANS FOR LAND AND DECISION CRITERIA

In order to analyze landowners' future plans, those conducting the survey asked landowners about the likelihood of taking certain actions within the next five years. Most landowners (65.2 percent) reported that they wanted to retain their property in its current use (see table 1.11). Interestingly, this number is quite consistent with the percentage of landowners who agreed that, given the choice, they would keep their land in its current use indefinitely (73.7 percent). If transfer of the property was contemplated, there was an equal inclination toward selling the property and giving the property to a family member. Cross-regional comparisons reveal a great deal of similarity. However, Sacramento landowners were significantly more likely to sell some of or all their property, develop the land themselves, or subdivide their property compared with landowners in the other three regions. It is interesting that large fringe landowners in Portland and Sacramento, the two western—and newer—cities in the sample, were less likely to commit to restricting land to current uses in perpetuity. Perhaps there is a western sensibility that shapes owner perspectives and attitudes.

The complexity and multiple motives of large fringe landowners are also evidenced by their responses when asked to rate the importance of various factors in their decisions and future plans regarding

Table 1.11   Future plans for land

	Austin	Charlotte	Portland	Sacramento	Total
Likely action in the next 5 years					
Retain current use	66.3	68.8	65.8	60.1	65.2
Purchase adjacent land	7.8	5.1	6.7	6.4	6.6
Sell property	15.3	18.1	18.8	24.8*	19.1
Give to relative	18.4	20.5	15.4	18.3	18.4
Develop the land and sell afterward	1.2	1.9	3.4	7.3*	3.3
Subdivide the property	3.5	3.7	5.4	16.5*	7.3
N	255	215	149	218	837
Percentage who would retain current use indefinitely					
Yes	82.3	77.6	65.8	65.1	73.7
No	15.4	19.2	31.5	31.7	23.5
Don't know/refused	2.4	3.3	2.7	3.2	2.9
N	254	214	149	218	835

Note: Likelihood is rated on a scale of 1 to 5. Percentages indicate those who rated the factor a 5 (highly likely). This survey question accepted multiple responses because owners may have separate plans for different portions of their land.
* Significantly different from all other regions at $p < 0.05$.

the property (see table 1.12). Overall, planning and policy factors, such as zoning and subdivision regulations, taxes, and environmental regulations, rated as the three most important factors. As might be expected, all the relevant taxes were important, but property taxes ranked slightly ahead of the others. Despite the key role of planning and policy, economic and quality-of-life considerations rated highly as well. Factors such as neighbors' land decisions; development pressures in the area; expected return on agriculture; and transportation, sewer, and water access all had similar importance: roughly 20 percent of landowners rated them as "very important." These results were quite consistent across regions, except that significantly more landowners were concerned about land regulations in Portland than in other regions. This is no doubt because land use regulations in Portland are more stringently imposed through growth-control policies.

In terms of making decisions, respondents showed some variation in their sophistication and use of tools to help them become more informed. Only 42 percent of large fringe landowners reported perform-

Table 1.12   Importance of various factors, taxes, and investment advice to owners in making land use decisions

	Austin	Charlotte	Portland	Sacramento	Total
Percentage who said factor was important					
Neighbors' land decisions	22.0	22.3	21.5	22.5	22.1
Development pressures	20.4	19.1	25.5	23.4	21.7
Expected return on agriculture	14.1	13.0	20.8	23.9	17.6
Zoning and subdivision regulations	22.4	30.2	45.6*	36.2	32.1
Environmental regulations	27.8	23.3	25.5	28.0	26.3
Taxes	32.9	34.0	22.1	27.1	29.7
Transportation access	18.8	21.4	18.1	17.9	19.1
Sewer and water access	20.4	25.1	18.8	17.4	20.5
Availability of optional conservation programs	10.2	12.1	7.4	6.9	9.3
N	255	215	149	218	837
Percentage who said tax was important					
Income	35.3	34.0	34.0	54.1	39.3
Capital gains	34.5	40.2	47.2	52.9	42.5
Gift and estate	38.8	47.4	41.5	55.3	45.6
Property	60.3	63.9	47.2	62.4	59.8
N	116	97	53	85	351
Land investment analysis Percentage who					
Regularly analyze land investments	41.2	38.1	41.6	48.6	42.4
Have ever sought advice or assistance in analyzing land investments	28.6	27.0	32.2	33.0	30.0
Have ever sought advice from an estate planner	27.1	29.3	35.6	30.3	30.0
N	255	215	149	218	837
Percentage wishing to pass land on to heirs	79.9	82.9	75.5	78.9	79.7
N	254	211	143	209	817
Percentage who believe heirs will continue current land use	64.5	60.0	56.5	59.0	60.6
N	203	175	108	166	652

Note: For the factors and taxes, respondents were asked to rate importance on a scale of 1 to 5. For the factors, the table reports the percentage of respondents who rated the factor a 5. For taxes, the table reports the percentage of respondents who rated the factor a 4 or a 5.

* Significantly different from all other regions at $p < 0.05$.

ing regular land investment analysis, and only 30 percent had ever sought advice or assistance in analyzing land investments. In total, 52.2 percent either performed their own land investment analysis or sought some external advice regarding decisions about the future disposition of their parcels.

GENERAL PARTICIPATION IN LAND MARKET

Across regions, there were remarkable similarities in the percentages of landowners who owned other land in their respective metropolitan areas and in their propensity to buy or sell other properties (see table 1.13). Roughly 41 percent of landowners in each region owned other land in their MSA at the time of the survey. Unfortunately, the survey did not capture whether this other land was located at the fringe or in a suburban or urbanized area. Landowners in land-intensive professions such as farming, ranching, and real estate investment and development were significantly more likely to possess other land in their MSA than those who were retired or engaged in non-land-intensive professions. The median acreage of owners' other land was much larger in Sacramento than in other regions: Sacramento landowners were more likely to be large landowners in other contexts. More generally, though, these alternate parcels were smaller than the large parcels on the fringe that were the focus of the survey. Our large landholders on balance engaged the market on a larger scale through only a single land channel.

Overall, the reasons most frequently mentioned for owning other land were recreational or residential use, income-generating agriculture or other rural land uses, and investment purposes. However, the importance of these reasons varied significantly across the four regions. For example, Austin landowners were significantly more likely to possess other land for recreational or residential purposes compared with landowners from other regions, and Portland and Sacramento landowners were more likely to value income-generating agriculture or other rural land uses. In addition, although the percentage of landowners who possessed other land for investment purposes was quite similar across all four regions, prospective holding times were not. Landowners in Austin, Charlotte, and Sacramento were more likely to sell the other land within five years; Portland landowners were more likely to keep the other land for a longer period of time. Few large

Table 1.13   General land market participation

	Austin	Charlotte	Portland	Sacramento	Total
Percentage owning other land in metro area	41.6	38.1	44.3	41.3	41.1
Median acres, other land	20.0	15.0	15.0	100.0	21.0
N	255	215	149	218	837
Reasons for ownership (percentage)					
Recreational or residential use	52.3*	41.9	36.8	21.3*	38.6
Income from agriculture or other rural land uses	30.2	32.3	49.1*	58.7*	42.1
To develop land	3.5	8.1	5.3	12.0	7.1
Investment purposes	26.7	27.4	31.6	24.0	27.1
Selling within 5 years	16.3	14.5	12.3	16.0	15.0
Selling in 5 years or more	10.5	12.9	19.3	8.0	12.1
To protect land or other natural resources	3.5	6.5	8.8	1.3	4.6
N	86	62	57	75	280
Percentage currently looking to buy new parcels in area	18.0	19.1	16.1	17.9	17.9
N	255	215	149	218	837
Frequency of buying new parcel in area (percentage)					
Never buy land	62.4	65.1	55.7	55.5	60.1
Less than once per 6 years	26.3	21.4	28.9	28.0	25.9
At least once every 5 years	10.6	12.1	12.1	16.1	12.7
Don't know/refused	0.8	1.4	3.4	0.5	1.3
N	255	215	149	218	837
Percentage currently looking to sell other parcels in metro area (only owners who own other land)	36.8	35.4	25.8*	36.7	34.3
N	106	82	66	90	344
Frequency of selling other land in area (percentage)					
Never buy land	69.8	72.1	71.1	67.0	69.9
Buy land less than once per 6 years	22.0	19.5	24.2	17.4	20.5
Buy land at least once every 5 years	6.7	8.4	4.7	14.7	8.8
Don't know/refused	1.6	0.0	0.0	0.9	0.7
N	255	215	149	218	837

Note: Area is metropolitan area. Count (N) of reasons for ownership excludes those who did not mention any of the five reasons listed in the table, regardless of whether the owner specified other reasons or answered "don't know/refused."

* Significantly different from all other regions at $p < 0.05$.

fringe landowners (4.6 percent) reported that they possessed other land in order to protect land or other natural resources—a finding consistent with earlier observations.

Overall, the large fringe landowners were only occasional participants in land markets via other properties. Over 85 percent of respondents reported that they either never or relatively rarely bought or sold other land, and only 10 percent reported engagement at frequencies higher than once every five years. Less than 18 percent of large fringe landowners were seeking to buy other properties, and only 34 percent of those who owned other properties were seeking to sell them. Few differences were seen across regions.

OWNER PERCEPTIONS OF GROWTH

Given the ongoing debate about urban expansion and sprawl, a final set of survey questions focused on perceptions of local development and the potential effects on issues such as land values, property taxes, options for land, open space and scenery, and quality of life (see table 1.14). The responses make clear that landowners viewed these lands as being at the urban fringe. A majority of respondents reported living in a rural-suburban mix. In addition, sizable numbers of respondents living in what they characterized as a rural area reported seeing evidence of increasing suburban infringement—in the form of infrastructure and housing—into their area. The large fringe landowners also noted that their land was being priced at levels above typical farmland valuations, which suggests that the market views these parcels as a blend of the rural and the urban.

Perhaps most interesting are the attitudes toward development that were observed among these large fringe landowners. There was a clear ambivalence toward development. These owners recognized that development would increase land values, and by extension wealth, and generally believed that development would not weaken community linkages and cohesion. At the same time, the owners also worried that development would degrade the natural scenery and environmental quality, diminish the viability of agricultural lifestyles, and increase property taxes.

On balance, there does not appear to be a clear consensus about development among large fringe landowners who have seen some devel-

Table 1.14   Owners' perceptions of development in their area

	Austin	Charlotte	Portland	Sacramento	Total
Percentage who describe their area currently as					
Rural	39.2	12.6*	21.5	34.9	28.1
Mostly rural	51.4	60.0*	50.3	43.1	51.3
Mostly suburban	7.8*	25.1	26.8	21.1	19.1
Don't know/refused	1.6	2.3	1.3	0.9	1.6
N	255	215	149	218	837
If rural or mostly rural, percentage who have not seen signs of development in the past 5 years	6.5	2.6*	6.5	8.8	6.2
Percentage seeing land values higher than usual in farm-to-farm sales	72.3	77.6	66.4	69.4	71.8
Percentage seeing higher-value agriculture/hobby farms/ranches replacing existing farms or ranches	57.6	50.6	57.9	51.8	54.5
Percentage seeing construction of infrastructure for suburban-style development	61.9	78.2	67.3	52.4	64.2
Percentage seeing new suburban-style development on former farmland or open space	74.9	85.9	77.6	67.6	76.1
N	231	156	107	170	664
Of those who have seen signs of development, percentage believing that if development continued at current pace, it would be likely to increase the following in the next 5 years					
Land values	86.2	86.7	79.6	83.7	84.5
Property taxes	84.9	83.4	73.2	60.1	76.1
Options for land	42.3	45.0	33.1	43.3	41.6
Difficulty to conduct agriculture	56.5	69.2	57.0	65.0	62.1
Loss of open space and scenery	70.3	69.2	67.6	64.0	67.9
Degradation of environmental quality	61.9	56.9	58.5	45.8	55.8
Weakening sense of community	29.3	39.3	35.2	32.0	33.7
Degradation of quality of life	41.4	44.1	51.4	41.9	44.0
N	239	211	142	203	795

Note: The second "N" includes only those landowners who described their area currently as rural or mostly rural. The total number of landowners who had seen signs of development includes (1) landowners who described their area currently as rural or mostly rural and have seen signs of development; and (2) landowners who described their area currently as mostly suburban. Infrastructure includes new roads, sewers, and water connections.

* Significantly different from all other regions at $p < 0.05$.

opment in their area.[3] About 44 percent of respondents who had seen development believed that the development would degrade the quality of life in the region. Only in Portland, where policies have been adopted to limit such development, did this proportion exceed 50 percent. Large fringe landowners seemed to mirror the conflicted view of the general population regarding development on the fringe. This suggests that future development on the fringe will continue to occur in fits and starts as individual large landowners make their own, somewhat idiosyncratic, decisions about whether and how to develop their lands.

Comparison of Large Holders with Other Fringe Holders

An important question is whether large fringe landowners differ from their smaller counterparts, a question that can be assessed by comparing the findings here with those in Molinsky's study (2006), which evaluated owners of fringe lands of five acres or larger in the same four MSAs. We see that large fringe landowners had very similar characteristics to the smaller fringe landholders in terms of age, gender, race, education, income, and wealth. However, we do observe some significant differences. Large fringe landowners were more likely than owners of smaller parcels to have received their land through inheritance and less likely to have purchased it directly. Among those who purchased their land, large owners cited suitability for agriculture or ranching as a motivation significantly more frequently than did smaller owners. Consequently, it is not surprising that large fringe lands are more likely to be used for agricultural purposes and less likely to be used for nonfarm residential or open space purposes than smaller parcels on the fringe. In addition, significantly more large owners reported that they regularly analyze land investments or seek advice or assistance in analyzing land investments. We also find that a significantly higher percentage of large landowners owned other land in the metro area. These statistics suggest that large owners are more likely to make decisions regarding their land in light of business considerations than owners of smaller plots.

3. Landowners who had seen signs of development consisted of two groups: landowners who described their area currently as rural or mostly rural and landowners who described their area currently as mostly suburban.

In terms of participation in land markets, large fringe landowners were significantly more likely to have received previous offers to purchase or develop. However, this greater pressure did not translate into a greater willingness on the part of large landowners to engage the local land market. Compared with smaller owners, only a slightly larger percentage of large owners were currently interested in selling or transferring their property. Perhaps this finding is related to similarities in the initial motivations owners had for acquiring the land: similar percentages of large and small landowners initially intended to subdivide, develop, or hold and then sell their land. As for their future plans, a slightly smaller percentage of large owners planned to hold the property in its current use, and the same percentage wished to purchase surrounding land. Slightly more planned to sell some of or all their property, and slightly more wanted to give property to a family member.

When asked about the various factors that influence their decisions on how to manage their land, large landowners reported that they were slightly less concerned about their neighbors' land decisions. This may be because, given their greater propensity to have an operating business, they place greater weight on individual profit motives than on less concrete social benefits and costs. Large fringe landowners also reported that they were more concerned about the expected return on agriculture and environmental regulatory restrictions—which is consistent with this possible explanation and the observed land use differences. However, survey responses suggest that large landowners are not monolithic, as they were also less likely than smaller owners to be concerned about taxes and were comparably likely to want to pass their land on to children or other family members.

Conclusions

In this chapter we study the characteristics, behaviors, interests, and intentions of large fringe landowners, especially their decisions regarding land use, subdivision, development, sale, and transfer. Overall, the survey indicates that large fringe landowners are not monolithic, but rather are a complex group. They are driven by multiple motivations in deciding whether and how to supply their lands for urban development and continued growth. Business profits, investment returns, planning rules, quality-of-life considerations, and bequest motives all play important roles. These results suggest that development at the fringe will not happen smoothly, but rather will occur in fits and starts depending on which large fringe landowners control which parcels.

Moreover, we observe that large fringe landowners differ from owners of small parcels at the fringe. They are more likely to be business-oriented and tend to face more development pressure. However, this does not appear to translate into a greater propensity to sell or transfer their land.

Most of our findings are consistent across the fringes of Austin, Charlotte, Portland, and Sacramento. Although these four regions have different histories, geographies, economies, and policies, all are experiencing rapid population growth. We find that fringe lands in these four areas are currently mostly used for agriculture or remain undeveloped. A significant percentage of the large fringe landowners wished to keep their land in its current use and pass it on to their children or other family members in the future, whereas a significant minority of owners planned to sell, transfer, develop, or subdivide part of or all their land within five years. There are few consistent predictors regarding ownership patterns or owners' interests and decisions. Interestingly, a clear group of investors or land speculators did not emerge in any region.

However, regional differences do exist. Portland has a special planning and policy context among the four regions because of its stringent land use regulations and rigorously applied growth-control policies. Given the suitability of its land for farming, Sacramento has a long tradition in agriculture. Charlotte has a long tradition in land legacy, and its current fringe landowners are more likely to pass their land on to their children or other family members than to sell or develop it. These historical, geographical, economic, and regulatory differences underlie some disparities in large fringe landowners' behaviors and their general participation in the land market.

An important caveat is that there is no guarantee that landowners will behave in the future as they responded in the survey. However, we observed considerable consistency in responses to many questions across the four MSAs, which provides some confidence in the stability of observed relationships. In addition, there is always the possibility that unforeseen events, ranging from life-cycle issues to attractive offers from buyers, will change large fringe landowners' future plans and behavior. Although this is a shortcoming of all survey approaches, readers should keep such limitations in mind.

2

CUSTOMARY LANDHOLDERS AND THE PLANNING PROCESS IN CONTEMPORARY ENUGU, NIGERIA

Cosmas Uchenna Ikejiofor

The process of urbanization is one of the most important dimensions of economic, social, and physical change in Africa. Approximately 25 percent of continental Africa's population lived in towns and cities in 1975 (UNCHS 1996, 4). In 2000, because of the combined effects of rural-urban migration and rapid rates of natural increase, 38 percent of the continent's population lived in urban areas, and the proportion is expected to increase to 47 percent by 2015 (UNCHS 2001, 271). Buckley and Kalarickal (2005) project that half the world's poor (a substantial proportion of whom are in Africa) are expected to be living in cities by 2035. The World Bank (1996) had projected that Nigeria's urban population of about 40 million would double in 13 years if the then-current growth rate of 5.5 percent persisted. Rapid urbanization means increasing demand for urban land, particularly for housing, but also for various other urban uses. Ensuring that urban land markets are managed efficiently to serve the economic and social needs of urban inhabitants and enterprises has thus become one of the most pressing issues in cities throughout the third world (UNCHS 1996).

In many African cities today, the land market consists of a combination of three or more systems of land supply: indigenous tenure, illegal modes, capitalist markets, and bureaucratic allocation procedures. These systems overlap, vary in their characteristics and interactions, and produce confused, complex patterns of land supply (Simon 1992). However, there is a consensus in much of the literature that the indigenous communal land tenure system provides the bulk of land for urban development in many African cities (Acquaye and Asiama 1986; Frishman 1988; Van Westen 1990; Mabogunje 1992; Dale 1997).

Concerning the impact of this dominant source of land supply on the urban planning process, analysts observe that actors in the informal (customary) sector have begun to develop practices that can overcome the problems of informal land supply. These practices include attempts by community leaders to foster orderly layouts, register land transfers, develop guarantees of tenure security, and service land. In addition, an intricate set of relationships between government agencies, formal land institutions, and indigenous landowning groups has evolved. The key theoretical significance of these developments is the challenge that they pose to the conventional conceptualization of urban land delivery systems in African cities in terms of two distinct categories: "formal" and "informal." They also highlight the problems associated with the current practice of employing dichotomist terms (such as "legal" and "illegal," "formal" and "informal," "regular" and "irregular," "planned" and "unplanned," and "secure" and "insecure") in describing these systems. From their analysis of experience and evidence from South Africa, Cousins and others (2005) conclude that the entire legal and social complex around which notions of "formal" and "informal" property are constituted needs to be examined more vigorously. Rakodi (2006, 264) alludes to the accommodative tactics adopted by both state and nonstate actors in land delivery systems in Africa.

The African experience of rapid urbanization under conditions of widespread poverty is, in practice, based on a delicate amalgam of individual interests, social control by local communities, passive tolerance by the "absent" central state, and active tolerance or outright assistance by local government, the legal sector (e.g., courts of law), public and private utility companies, foreign donors, and nongovernmental organizations (Olima and Kreibich 2002, 4). Royston and others (2005, 13), calling for a review of tenure terminology and concepts, observe that dichotomy is problematic because it indicates false polarization, more appropriately represented as a continuum in which the situation is moving toward more informality or formality.

Views on how best to manage African land markets range from arguments in favor of maintaining communal tenure to arguments for its abolition and transition to individual titles. Some of the literature argues that "informality" and illegality reduce the costs of land and housing for the urban poor. Others argue that as long as the poor are insecure regarding the legal status of their homes (their major assets in life), they will never enjoy full access to the economic and political system (see, e.g., De Soto 2000).

Relying on a 2006 study of the impact of customary landholding on emerging land markets in Enugu funded by the Lincoln Institute of Land Policy (Ikejiofor 2007) as well as on secondary sources and personal observations, I aim to highlight in this chapter the essential role that dominant customary landholders play in emerging land markets, particularly in the context of land assembly for urban development, and their overall impact on the planning process. First, I provide some background on the development of Enugu as well as on the land transfer process in the city. This is followed by an in-depth analysis of the emerging land markets and the concepts, actors, and roles involved in customary landholding in the Enugu context. My discussion of the challenges and opportunities involved in accessing customary land for urban development looks specifically at the issue of tenure security in customary land and its impact on the activities of private developers and government agencies saddled with formal land administration in Enugu. For details of the methodology employed in data collection for the study, see Ikejiofor (2007).

The Development of Enugu

Enugu, which literally means hilltop, derives its name from its position among the Udi hills at an altitude of about 223 meters above mean sea level. It is located between latitudes 6° 27′ N and 7° 28′ N and longitude 7° 30′ E and 8° 19′ E (Government of Anambra State 1978, 41). Enugu covers an area of about 72.4 square kilometers at the foothills of the Udi escarpment, and the surrounding rural areas (now being transformed into settlement centers) cover an area of about 200 square kilometers (Ezeh 1998, 3; Government of Anambra State 1978, 39). The discovery of coal in the area in 1909 and the subsequent construction of a railway played critical roles in the town's evolution. The

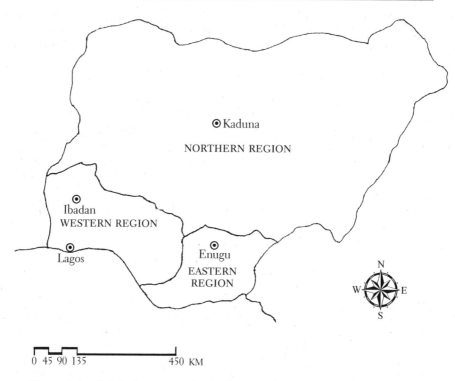

Figure 2.1   Political map of Nigeria showing defunct regional structure.
Barbour et al. (1982, 29)

capital of the defunct Eastern Region, Enugu has remained a very important administrative, industrial, and commercial center in the eastern parts of southern Nigeria, but it has continued to suffer territorial loss over the years as a result of the creation of nine states (over time) out of the former Eastern Region (see figures 2.1 and 2.2). It is at present split into three local government councils: Enugu North, Enugu South, and Enugu East.

Urban Population and Growth Trends

According to the 2006 national census, Enugu had a total population of 722,664 in 28 residential settlements. Documentary evidence indicates that the population increased from 3,170 in 1926 to 13,600 in 1931, to 62,764 in 1953, to 138,457 in 1963, to 166,541 in 1978, to 342,786 in 1986, and to 465,072 in 1991. Between 1991 and 2006, the population of Enugu grew at about 3 percent per annum.

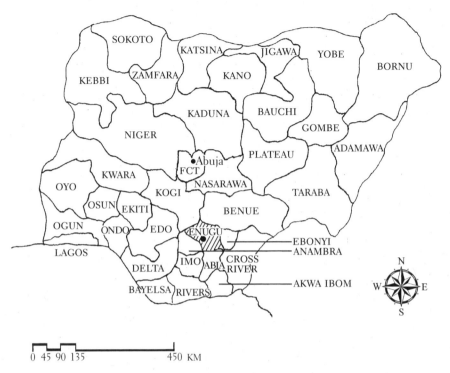

Figure 2.2   Political map of Nigeria showing state boundaries and the location of Enugu in Enugu state. *Modified from Barbour et al. (1982, 29)*

The Land Transfer Process

Supply-side agents in the Enugu land transfer process include indigenous customary landowners (acting through their headmen), the government, private individuals (who may be speculators), and middlemen. Indigenous customary landowners dominate the supply side of the land market, the bulk of land for transfer existing in insipient peripheral settlements. The government and private individual developers or speculators operate on the demand side. Tenure characteristics in land transactions differ, but leasehold—the only mode of land ownership recognized by the 1978 Land Use Decree—has come to dominate in recent times. Although the decree specifies a statutory leasehold of 99 years on government land, leases on customary land are often shorter.

There are notions of winners and losers and costs and benefits in the land transfer process in Enugu. According to Mbiba and Huch-zermeyer (2002, 121), winners are often the local elites—officials, politicians, and headmen—who exploit their access to resources and their ability to dictate land entitlements. The major cost of peri-urban transformation in Enugu can be observed in the environmental impact of water consumption, waste disposal, noise, and traffic. The distributional impact of these environmental problems confirms that there are losers in the land transfer process. On the other hand, key benefits of the process are employment generation and wealth creation.

Emerging Land Markets in Enugu: Actors and Motives

Categorizing Emerging Land Markets

Land markets in Enugu may be categorized in terms of the prevailing systems of supply. These different modes of supply originated at different stages in the city's development. When land markets are approached from this perspective, three categories of suppliers of land for conversion from rural to urban uses can be identified: the traditional authority figures (clan heads, village heads, lineage heads, family heads, or their representatives); land subdividers (speculators); and the government and its agencies. The volume of supply from each category is directly related to the amount of land under its rule. Although figures are not available, it is reasonable to assume that land in Enugu is held in the following proportions: customary land rights owners hold 80 percent; the public sector, 10 percent; and private individuals, 10 percent. I shall briefly explain the assumptions upon which this conjecture is based. As earlier mentioned, the original urban boundary of Enugu covers an area of about 72 square kilometers, and the surrounding villages (which are rapidly being incorporated into the urban boundary) provide an additional 200 square kilometers. Most of the land in the surrounding villages is under indigenous occupation, and at least one-third of the land (including vast areas in Ogui Nike and Awkunanaw) within the original urban boundary is still under customary ownership.

Consequently, the first and the most important of the land market categories (in terms of the number of plots supplied) are the indigenous communities and landowning families acting through their representatives. By way of comparison, although there was no government land delivery program in Enugu in the whole of 2005, figures gleaned from the register of alienated communal land in the Enugu study show that in 2005 alone, over 700 plots were sold by the various landowning families. Past studies (e.g., Okolocha 1993; Ikejiofor 1997) show that this source of supply accounts for most of the land that is made available for urban development in other Nigerian cities. But because transactions in this segment of the market are not officially recognized, they yield little or no revenue to the government. I provide a detailed discussion of the nature and dynamics of this dominant mode of land supply in the Enugu context later in this chapter.

The second category of land markets in Enugu involves the mostly nonindigenous land subdividers or speculators. This segment of the private land delivery system refers to the activities of private actors who obtain land mostly from customary sources, subdivide the land, develop some plots, and resell the remainder to the public. Because this group of suppliers consists mostly of speculators, this group often acquires cheap peripheral land and then waits until urban expansion reaches those areas before selling. Hence, land from this source is often not appropriately located. The limited number of such actors in operation also restricts the volume of supply relative to demand. Depending on the legality of the subdivider, tenure security here may be better guaranteed than in the informal (indigenous supply) system because the terms of a particular land transfer are clear, unambiguous, and often properly documented. Such documentary evidence (where it exists) is usually enforceable in the law courts.

The third category of land markets in Enugu involves public sector supply. The government and its agencies have played a significant role in both the supply and demand sides of the land market since colonial times. All three tiers of government (federal, state, and local) are involved. In Enugu, the government, among other things, continues to acquire land from customary and private sources for public use, supplies land to private individuals and groups from its pool, establishes rules regarding land use planning for economic development, provides infrastructure and services to land, and enforces development control laws. The Lands Division of the Ministry of Lands, Survey, and Town Planning carries out land acquisitions on behalf of the government. Figure 2.3 summarizes formal land administration in Enugu.

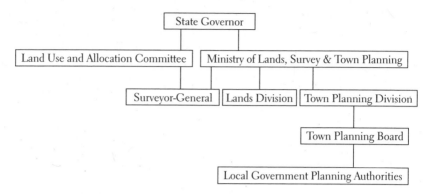

Figure 2.3   Organogram of formal land administration in Enugu. *Ikejiofor, Nwogu, and Nwanunobi (2004)*

There is no doubt that tenure security is guaranteed in the public land delivery system. The Land Use Decree of 1978 stipulated a lease-hold tenure of 99 years. It is this issue of tenure security that is perhaps the greatest attraction of the public land supply system. Anyone who is able to cross the allocation hurdle and pay the necessary fees is almost always assured of both de facto and de jure security in public residential layouts since that person receives a title document and a certificate of occupancy. Because the terms of the lease are clearly spelled out and are not subject to sudden changes, no allottee considers his ownership or control of the allotted land at risk as long as he does not default in paying the stipulated fees. There is a dearth of reliable data on how well plots in public residential layouts in Enugu do in providing a flow of revenue to the local governments, through property tax and user charges, for the provision of services. Past studies show, however, that the default rate in public land and housing supply programs is quite high (Agbola 1990).

It is important to note that the complexity reported by some analysts to dominate urban land tenure issues in the urban areas of most developing countries is largely absent in Enugu. This is because land invasion and squatting as a source of land supply for low-income groups rarely occurred in the past and certainly does not occur today. None of the respondents in the semistructured questionnaire survey of land purchasers in the Enugu study had obtained land through illegal occupation. The absence of squatting means that the usually complex varieties of nonformal tenure systems associated with it are largely absent in Enugu, whether we are looking at communal, private, or government-owned land. Hence, such informal tenure systems reported by Payne (1997, 8) to be the most common in developing countries, particularly in terms of providing land for low-income settlements, hardly exist in Enugu. This has adverse implications for market access, price trends, and affordability, particularly for those in the lower income brackets.

Formal Land Supply Prices and Their Impact on Land Values in Enugu

The inability or unwillingness of the public land supply system to meet demand was confirmed in an interview of officials of the Ministry of Lands, Survey, and Town Planning carried out as part of the Enugu study. The officials noted a lack of funds to embark on the acquisition, subdivision, servicing, and allocation of plots on a scale that would match the volume of demand. It was clear that targeting low-income earners in land allocation is not a priority for the ministry. The land delivery programs of the ministry operate strictly on a cash-and-carry basis—only those who can pay the price may participate.

Allottees of plots in government layouts in Enugu are required to pay 15 different categories of fees. As of December 2005, these fees included a nonrefundable application fee of N1000 (US$8), an approval fee of N5000 (US$40), a deed registration fee of N4000 (US$32), a consent fee of at least N5000 (US$40) for the preparation of a certificate of occupancy, a survey fee of N25000 (US$200), and a development premium (meant to enable the government to provide infrastructure in the layouts) calculated at a rate of N175 (US$1.40) per square meter.[1] Depending on the location, a standard high-density plot (20 x 30 square meters) would require a development premium of at least N105,000 (US$840). There is also the property rate (which is calculated on the basis of the status of the layout and the type of development) paid annually to the local government, and the ground rent of N7500 (US$60) per hectare paid annually to the state government in acknowledgment of the leasehold tenure. This rent is usually increased periodically.

1. As of December 2005, the exchange rate was US$1 for N125.

In Enugu, the annual take-home pay of an upper low-income civil servant in 2005 was about N120,000 (US$960), which is far less than the total fees charged for a standard high-density plot. Added to these fees are the political and human barriers introduced by policy and endemic corruption in the plot-allocation process. The absence of functional land and housing finance institutions and the poor savings mobilization capacity of most Nigerians (resulting from a harsh economic environment) mean that the obstacles are indeed insurmountable for most small developers and a vast majority of the population, who fall into the lower and middle income brackets.

The sites and services principle underlies most of the ministry's land delivery programs, but none have specifically targeted low-income people. The shortage of funds has meant that emphasis has always been on cost recovery, which puts low-income people at a disadvantage.

Because of the high cost of plots in government land-subdivision programs in Enugu, the type of active submarkets that usually develop around government land allocation systems (Durand-Lasserve 1994, 67) through the resale of plots is largely absent. Also, the high cost of plots in the formal submarket directly affects the cost of plots in the informal (customary) submarket, as will be argued shortly.

The Nature and Dynamics of Customary Landholding in Enugu

Customary Landholding: Concepts, Actors, and Roles

In Enugu, three systems of customary land ownership are evident: communal, family, and individual systems of land ownership. In former times, the greatest area of land was held by the community as communal land. But with an increasing population and the allotment of communal land to families, a gradual transformation of land from communal to family landholding has occurred. Communal landholding in the study area still exists in such places as farmlands, community squares and playgrounds, markets, and burial grounds, and accounts for about 20 percent of all customary land in Enugu. Family landholding accounts for almost the remaining 80 percent. Individual ownership of customary land is negligible and, in practice, occurs only temporarily as a transitory phase to formal registration of such land. McAuslan (1998, 543) notes that the creation of an individual right of occupancy and its allocation to an individual or group through a statutory process ipso facto breaks the link between the land and customary tenure, even if the same people occupy the land. Cousins and others (2005, 3) corroborate this view by observing that there is often a fundamental incompatibility between property rights in community-based systems and the requirements of formal property. The formalization (individualization) of communal property rights, they note, transforms and alters both the nature of the rights and the social relations and identities that underlie them. This, according to McAuslan (1998, 543), poses the greatest challenge to the evolution of customary tenure.

Family landholding implies that title to land is vested in the family. "Title," in this context, does not necessarily need to be supported with documentary evidence. All that is required for such title to exist is the verbal agreement of the recognized community leader (or council of elders) to allocate a particular piece of communal land to a particular family in the community for perpetuity. It is only a family wishing to formalize such title that must obtain this agreement in written form. This written agreement, together with a map of the plot prepared by a licensed surveyor, constitutes "proof" of rights to the land. This "proof" is what is presented to the relevant government agency for the issuance of a statutory lease (or certificate of occupancy) under the 1978 Land Use Decree. A certificate of occupancy issued in such circumstances can be inherited or transferred to a person outside the family or community for cash.

Family, strictly speaking, goes beyond the narrow English conception of a family comprising just father, mother, and children (nuclear family). In a Nigerian context, the family consists of the father, the mother, and their children, but also includes uncles, aunts, brothers, sisters, nieces, nephews, grandparents, and grandchildren. In the survey of heads of customary landowning families in Enugu, 90 percent of respondents indicated the same grandfather as the biological connection among members of their family (see table 2.1). All the respondents in the study identified inheritance as the means through which family land owned in common is passed down from the progenitor to the present generation of family members.

Land belonging to a family is normally held in trust for the members by the family head, who is the eldest male member of that family. Land ownership is seen as part of the *Nkolo* (symbol of family unity), and the eldest male member, who is also in charge of the *Ofo* (symbol

Table 2.1 Biological connection among indigenous family members in Enugu

Relationship	No. in sample	Percentage
Same father	1	2
Same grandfather	54	90
Same great-grandfather	5	8
Other	nil	0
Total	60	100

Source: Ikejiofor (2007).

of authority), exercises control. The title to family land is held by the male members of the family as a group: it is joint and indivisible; no part can be alienated absolutely by an individual male member without the consent of the other male members of the family (usually the principal members). It thus has some similarities with joint tenancy under English law. However, no male member can claim any portion of the family land as his own, and each member is as much entitled to possession of any part of the land as the others. There is also a distinction between family land and tenancy in common. A tenant in common, under English law, has a definite share, though undivided, which he can alienate or otherwise transfer inter vivos or at death. A cause of action is vested in him in his own right when there is an interference with the land, for that amounts to an interference with his interest and an infringement of his rights. A family member, on the other hand, has no alienable share in family property.

Classification of Customary Landholders

In Enugu there are indigenous and nonindigenous customary landholders. The indigenous customary landholders can further be broken down into two groups (see table 2.2):

1. Those who own only customary land inherited from forebears
2. Those who, in addition to owning customary land inherited from forebears, have also acquired customary land from other customary holders through purchase or pledge

This second category includes indigenous entrepreneurs (individuals or families) who demand land in exchange for financial or other forms of assistance they render to their fellow kinsmen in need.

From table 2.2 it is clear that the overwhelming majority of indigenous customary landholders in the survey sample (87 percent) are

Table 2.2   Classification of indigenous customary landholders in Enugu

Landholding family	No. in sample	Percentage	No. of plots held	Average no. of plots per family
Inheritor only	52	87	592	11.4
Inheritor-purchaser	8	13	107	13.4
Total	60	100	699	

Source: Ikejiofor (2007).

families who own only customary land inherited from forebears. Another significant inference one can draw from the table is that the ownership structure of customary land in Enugu is broad based. The average number of plots per inheritor-only family does not differ significantly from that for the inheritor-purchaser family. This may be due to the small number of land transfers through pledge or purchase that occur among members of the indigenous society. Indigenous landowning families or individuals who want to sell land would prefer to sell to nonindigenes because of the likelihood of making more money from such a transaction: market forces, rather than social considerations, usually determine the selling price in transactions with nonindigenes. The absence of a small number of dominant customary landholders means that monopolistic behavior is largely absent in these emerging markets. In other words, seldom are there so few customary landholders who want to sell that they can control prices. Customary landholders respond to the market, and they gear the location, size, and price of plots to what people demand.

The category of nonindigenous customary landholders refers to nonmembers of the indigenous society who own customary land acquired mostly through purchase from customary holders, but who have not obtained formal title to such land. This category mainly includes the nonindigenous entrepreneurs who are either private developers or speculators, or both. Because of the precariousness of market transactions in customary land, the prevalent practice is for nonindigenes who acquire customary land to quickly obtain formal title to such land since this is believed to guarantee tenure security. As a result, customary landholding by nonindigenes, just like customary landholding by individual members of the indigenous community described earlier, is usually a transitory phase, and, at any point in time, there are relatively few landholders in this category.

What development dynamics can we observe in the activities of indigenous and nonindigenous customary landholders, and how do these differ? Some insight might be gained from examining the perception of land typical of the two groups. Whereas the indigenous customary landholder usually sees land as a God-given, valuable, but dwindling natural resource that can be exchanged for cash, his nonindigenous counterpart sees land as a foundation for economic activity, a factor of production, and a target for investment, provided that security of tenure is assured. For this group, therefore, land tenure security provides an incentive for investment, an impetus for economic development.

Accessing Customary Land for Urban Development in Enugu: Challenges and Opportunities

Bringing Customary Land into the Market: Underlying Dynamics and Motives

The emergence of a market in land (which is a more recent development) provides the channel through which "strangers" get land in Enugu. The survey of heads of indigenous landowning families in the Enugu study revealed that 70 percent of respondents had sold part of their family land in the past. The survey also sought to find out what factors prompted the decision to sell at each point in time, the uses to which family members usually put proceeds from alienated communal land, and the impact of changing urban boundaries on processes of land delivery and development—that is, what relationships exist between buyers and sellers of land, on the one hand, and formal administrative powers (e.g., state and local government authorities), on the other.

Of the sales examined in the survey, 90 percent were distress sales, and the proceeds were put to two main uses: children's education and the extension or maintenance of an existing family house (see table 2.3). All the respondents indicated that only adult male family members took part in making the decision to sell. None of the respondents had problems reaching an agreement to sell with other family members, probably because the children that needed money for education were not just those of the head of the family. The family houses that needed extensions or maintenance provided free accommodation for an increasing population of family members, particularly those with little or no income who could not build or rent houses of their own. It is instructive that the decision to sell was made primarily because of the need to deploy family wealth (land) into new areas of investment. All the respondents believed that it was the right decision. If their children received a good education, they could get good jobs, and that would more than compensate for the alienated land.

None of the respondents provided any form of infrastructure or services to the land before it was sold. Such lands were usually surveyed subsequently by licensed surveyors at the request of the purchasers. Because the plots that landowners were usually willing to sell at any one time were small, subdivision of plots by buyers for resale rarely occurred. This finding is also attributable to the fact that, apart from a few speculators, most of those who buy land do so with a view toward developing such land as an investment and bequeathing it to offspring. The size of a "standard" plot offered for sale is usually about 20 x 30 square meters. Only 5 percent of respondents in the survey had subdivided their plots since purchase (see table 2.4).

Proceeds from land sales are not taxed by either the state or the local government, since these formal administrative bodies do not usually get involved in private land transactions and are almost always unaware of such transactions. This stems from the lack of recognition of such transactions by the government and differs remarkably from the

Table 2.3   Use of proceeds from sale of family land in Enugu

Use	No. in sample	Percentage
Investment in children's education	24	40
Capitalization of microenterprises	12	20
Extension/maintenance of existing family house	18	30
Fulfillment of one-time social obligation (e.g., marriage, title-taking)	6	10
Total	60	100

Source: Ikejiofor (2007).

Table 2.4   Subdivision of plots after purchase in Enugu

Response	No. in sample	Percentage
Yes	3	5
No	50	83
No response	7	12
Total	60	100

Source: Ikejiofor (2007).

system in Ghana, where the traditional system is formally recognized and incorporated into the formal system and there is a formula for sharing revenue from land owned by indigenous, related groups led by a traditional authority figure (individually known as "stool") among the relevant "stool" and different layers of formal government (Gough and Yankson 2000, 2489). None of the customary landowner respondents in the Enugu study had paid any form of tax on proceeds from land sales; 70 percent argued that proceeds from land sales are not taxable, whereas 20 percent said that they were not aware of the requirement to pay tax (see table 2.5). None of the customary landowner respondents sought any form of permission from the government before embarking on the sale of land, because they believed that it was not the business of government what they did with their land.

However, those who buy land pay development levies and property taxes and are required to obtain building permits from the local planning authority for their projects. A development levy is the fee charged by the local government through its planning authority for all new developments in its area of jurisdiction. This levy often must be paid before a building permit is issued. The property tax, on the other hand, is the annual payment that all owners of developed property make to the local government in which such property is located. Both payments are made by all those who buy land, whether from state, customary, or other private sources. These levies are fixed by the local governments.

In most cases, as soon as a buyer purchases land and begins to develop that land, officials of the local planning authority visit the site with an order to stop work. The developer must pay the required levies before resuming work. This was the case even before 1991, when the Enugu metropolis was still a single local government area.

It is evident from the foregoing that private sector–led development in the peri-urban areas of Enugu usually precedes formal planning.

Table 2.5 Reasons for nonpayment of tax on land sales proceeds in Enugu

Response	No. in sample	Percentage
Tax not required	42	70
Proceeds insufficient to pay tax	3	5
Unaware of the requirement to pay tax	12	20
No response	3	5
Total	60	100

Source: Ikejiofor (2007).

Customary landholders provide the basic layout of residential settlements (indicating plot boundaries, the location of access roads, open and recreational spaces, etc.), and basic infrastructure and services (such as access roads, electricity, and potable water) are often provided by the developers themselves. By the time the local planning authority steps in, important planning decisions about the development have already been made by nonstate actors (in this case, customary landholders and private developers). Formal planning decisions in this situation necessarily have to accommodate these basic inputs from nonstate actors. The perception of a project's success or failure often depends critically on how well this intersection of planning and market forces is managed by public and private sector players.

Tenure Security in Customary Land: Impact on the Activities of Private Developers and Government Agencies

Why do plots sold by customary rights owners in Enugu often come in standard (formal) sizes? This trend can be traced to the precariousness of market transactions in customary land (resulting mostly from a lack of trust between parties), which creates a strong desire in most purchasers to obtain formal titles to such land from appropriate government agencies. Title to land can afford the protection of the formal courts of law in the event of a dispute. Hence, most purchasers of customary land often insist that the plots they buy meet the minimum size requirements for formal registration and titling. It would seem, therefore, that the cost barriers to land acquisition are a product of the cost of the land itself as well as bureaucratic obstacles (Ikejiofor 2006). This tendency of land purchasers has conditioned the behavior of customary landowners who, from long practice, are now quite astute in estimating the size of their landholding as multiples of the standard formal plot.

Findings from the Enugu study confirm the commonly held view that urban peripheral settlements are zones of active conversions of land from rural to urban uses. It has also been established that the bulk of land in such peripheral settlements is effectively in the hands of indigenous landowning communities and families. All the customary landowners who have sold part of their family land to buyers outside their families indicated that the prices at which plots were sold were determined solely by market forces.

Thus, purchasers of peripheral land, obtained at a market price from customary owners, usually register such land with public sector agencies in order to obtain formal title to the land, which is believed to enhance tenure security. Additional costs are usually incurred in the process of affecting such registration, further driving up the total cost of the land to the purchaser. Such additional costs include official taxes, levies, and administrative costs (such as deed fees, approval fees, survey check fees, inspection fees, stamp duties, and publication fees). There are also illicit payments and bribes demanded by some government officials, which, in some cases, may be greater than the taxes legally levied by the state. Hence, the total cost of land to the purchaser has two components: the price paid to the customary landowner and the costs (both official and illicit) incurred in registering the land.

The key issue here seems to be the low level of tenure security that land purchasers associate with customary land rights, demonstrated by the unwillingness of such purchasers to hold land for any length of time with the customary rights that are transferred to them when they buy land from indigenous owners. Such customary rights are usually not clearly defined; overlapping rights exist, and contracts are often unenforceable. As a result, transaction costs are high, and the residual risk of other claims coming to light following a sale decreases the value of the land and deters investment. All these factors, plus the fact that customary tenure rights cannot be used as collateral for loans from formal financial institutions, have led purchasers to accord customary rights of occupancy an inferior status vis-à-vis statutory rights. The failure of customary land rights owners in Enugu to develop acceptable guarantees of tenure security has thus become an inhibiting factor that has held down the value of customary land.

In Enugu, what an individual who wants a formal title on land acquired from customary sources must do depends on whether the land in question is in an approved layout. If it is in an approved layout, the individual applies to the Lands Division of the Ministry of Lands, Survey, and Town Planning; otherwise, the application is made to the Land Use and Allocation Committee in the office of the governor. In either case, the surveyor general is required to check and authenticate the plan of the plot before verifying the status of the land. In carrying out this verification, the presiding agency often consults the landowning community from which the applicant obtained the land and refers to the community's land register (i.e., the register of alienated communal lands that most landowning communities and families in Enugu keep) to establish proof of rights to the land. This is then followed by title registration or a recommendation to the governor that a certificate of occupancy be issued (or both). Verification of land status thus represents an area where a functional interface between formal and informal (customary) land management practices has emerged in Enugu.

The difference between the total cost of a plot to a purchaser and the price of the same plot in the customary market reflects the additional costs incurred in registering the plot. The purchaser of a plot who decides not to register the land can keep most of this difference if he is lucky or has the right contacts. A purchaser may, on the other hand, have to pay more than the total cost for the plot, especially if there is a legal dispute regarding the ownership of the plot. Registering the land, the costs of which most purchasers are usually willing to incur, takes care of this risk factor.

What factors determine the price at which customary rights owners are usually willing to sell land in Enugu? I have already mentioned that the broad-based nature of customary landholding in Enugu eliminates monopolistic tendencies and price volatility in the emerging land markets. Thus, although demand pressures are important explanatory factors, the selling price of plots in government layouts also plays a significant role, as indicated previously. It is this price that usually gives a customary rights owner an indication of the starting price at which to commence bargaining with a potential buyer. Because of this widespread practice of taking price signals from the selling price of government plots, it can be argued that some form of coordination mechanism exists among customary landholders.

Smolka (2003, 5) identified this interdependency of formal and informal urban land markets as a factor contributing to high land prices. Specifically, according to Smolka, the high prices of serviced land in the formal market seem to affect the relatively high prices of unserviced land in the informal market, and vice versa. According to Durand-Lasserve (1994, 61), the price of urban land is always established in relation to a so-called reference price, the ceiling to which all urban agents refer and the price used in the very narrow market for the resale of registered and legally occupied plots. Durand-Lasserve observed in the case of Conakry, Guinea, that the reference prices of plots differed from the prices charged in the customary market by about 20 to 30 percent when facilities and location were held constant. This price difference varies, it would seem, according to the degree of risk attached to owning customary land and the amount of trust placed in the customary owners. The price difference would widen if, for instance, the authorities had a repressive land development policy.

In the Enugu context, purchasers' lack of faith in customary land rights can result in a difference of up to 30 to 40 percent between the reference price and the price in the customary market. However, the fact that most land purchasers do not resell plots means that the submarket for the sale of fully titled private land is indeed very narrow. Evidence from the Enugu study indicates that even among the relatively few professional subdividers (speculators), it is only in very few cases that land is fully registered before resale. The passive tolerance of transactions in customary land and, to some extent, informal land development by the government has a moderating influence on the reference price.

Conclusion

The widespread instances of adaptation and accommodation between public and private actors in land delivery and development in contemporary Enugu suggests a flexible planning process. These instances also point to the fact that urban planning and management must be regarded not as a solely public sector activity, but as a partnership in which the search for an appropriate allocation of responsibility is continuing. The scope and potential for management by communities of their immediate living environments (especially land resources) must be given serious consideration; but we must also acknowledge that decisions about citywide infrastructure and the direction of future growth, planning for large-scale industry and transportation, and the allocation of resources between communities are better handled by the government because of the large economies of scale often involved.

II

ECONOMIC PRODUCTIVITY

3

THE NEIGHBORHOOD DYNAMICS OF HOSPITALS AS LARGE LANDOWNERS

Raphael W. Bostic, LaVonna B. Lewis, and David C. Sloane

The Hospital as an Institution

An enormous engine that consumes over 14 percent of the U.S. gross domestic product (GDP), the health care industry ranges from pharmaceutical and biotechnological companies on the cutting edge of research to family physicians in offices scattered throughout our communities. A recent study showed that the health care industry, in addition to its obvious importance to individual and public health, is crucial to metropolitan economies (DeVol et al. 2003). This study places Boston, New York, Philadelphia, Chicago, and Los Angeles as metropolitan leaders in the health care economy because of the range and depth of their activities.

The hospital plays a central and multifaceted role in the health care economy. First, hospitals are large employers. For instance, Cedars-Sinai Medical Center in Los Angeles "is the anchor [for] office[s] and [medical] clinics [that have] 8,600 on staff" (DeVol et al. 2003). Hospital employment is only the tip of the iceberg: medical centers such as Cedars-Sinai are often surrounded by other businesses related to the hospital's mission. Hospitals thus can be important for a community's economic performance, development, and stability.

Second, hospitals often serve as a focal point for ancillary health

We acknowledge financial support from the USC Lusk Center for Real Estate and the Lincoln Institute of Land Policy. We would like to thank John Karevoll and Dataquick for providing data, Xiaoxin Zhang for producing the maps, and Hina Gupta for research assistance. A special thanks is extended to Megan Cummings, Pria Hidisyan, Leza Mikhail, Katie Peterson, Lauren Siniawer, and Joshua Williams for their work as census surveyors.

care businesses, including physicians and other practitioners; medical specialists; and supportive services such as physical therapy, testing labs, and medical supply companies (Freeman, Sidhu, and Montoya 2006). These complementary activities are essential if a hospital is to have maximal effectiveness, and proximity can further enhance its efficacy. Thus, the demands of these ancillary businesses for space and buildings can potentially affect local land markets in important ways. Driving around virtually any urban hospital, one will find a constellation of other health care services (see figure 3.1). Some will be in commercial rental space, others in buildings that the hospital constructs to improve the efficiency of care for its patients and to provide complementary space for its affiliated health care providers.

Third, because of their role as an important provider of health care services, hospitals are a neighborhood amenity. As with all amenities, the additional benefits of hospitals are capitalized into the value of land near the hospital. Hospitals therefore influence land values in the neighborhoods in which they are located and can differentiate some neighborhoods and communities from others.

Figure 3.1 Example of surrounding medical uses, Westwood Surgery Center. *Photograph by David C. Sloane*

Hospitals in a Neighborhood Context

Finally, and importantly, hospitals are significant institutions for their surrounding neighborhoods because of their role as large landowners. Modern urban hospitals no longer occupy as much land as they did in the late nineteenth century, when concerns about cross-infection mandated pavilion-styled hospitals that could spread over dozens of acres. Advances in health care technology have allowed hospitals to deliver quality services with a smaller amount of land than they once required. Hospitals instead have become centers for a wide range of medical services, including ambulatory care, imaging and diagnosis, and traditional inpatient services. The result has been that hospitals often spread out, appropriating land around them for both current uses and future expansion. Some hospitals, such as Dartmouth-Hitchcock Medical Center, which is located on a 225-acre site in Lebanon, New Hampshire, have created large landholdings for future development. Urban hospitals rarely have such a luxury, but some have met the community's growing needs for health care services through a combination of in-fill construction on their existing campuses and the purchase or construction of buildings adjacent to the campus (see figure 3.2). In either instance, hospitals span a considerable area and are generally among the largest landowners in their communities.

Despite their obvious salience in terms of the size of their landholdings, hospitals have been understudied from a geographic and land use perspective. For example, DeVol and others (2003) note that "remarkably little quantification of the economic geography of health in the United States" has been reported in the scholarly literature. Health care scholars have traditionally focused on individual economies of health, particularly related to insurance, and the internal distribution of health care expenditures among the various activities of the industry. Notably, the expanded use of prescription drugs and the rise in drug prices have led to a deep literature on prescription drugs. Geography and space have been minor issues in this literature. Similarly, urban and real estate economists, who are more naturally disposed to consider space, have tended to focus on sectors, such as residential and retail, rather than on industries, such as health, whose land use cuts across those sectors.

Recently, that gap in the literature has slowly begun to fill as a growing body of work looks at the economic impacts of hospitals in Cali-

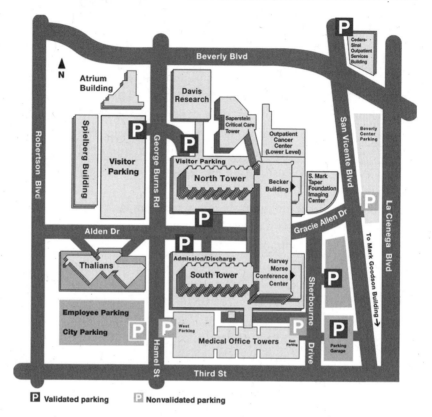

Figure 3.2   Cedars-Sinai campus map. © 2008 Cedars-Sinai Medical
Centers. All rights reserved. Reprinted with permission.

fornia, with particular attention paid to Los Angeles County. The
primary reason for this focus is that hospitals in California are under stress for a variety of reasons: limited (often negative) net operating margins, low reimbursement rates for government programs, un-
funded mandates such as seismic retrofitting and nurse staffing ratios,
uninsured and underinsured patients, and the continuing demand for
services. Elected officials, health foundations, and representatives of
the hospital industry have all been interested in examining how hospitals have handled these various stressors and the consequences when
hospitals are unable to handle them.

These studies have varied in their focus. One area of study has been
the impact of hospital closures (Scheffler et al. 2001). In this study, the
authors note that from 1995 to 2000, urban Southern California hospitals located in close proximity to other hospitals were most frequently

the ones that closed. The authors also report an acceleration in closures: more than twice as many occurred in the second half of the period studied as in the first. Finally, the authors note that hospitals with fewer than 100 licensed beds closed more often than any other type of hospital. A second study provides evidence that the closure of hospitals in Los Angeles County has reduced access and increased mortality for individuals residing in surrounding zip codes (Buchmueller, Jacobson, and Wold 2004).

A second area of study is the impact of emergency department closures and diversions on other area hospitals and communities (Melnick et al. 2004). Here, the focus was more on how the closures and diversions affected the organizational capacity and finances of the other hospitals. Although the authors conclude that the hospital emergency departments in California have maintained capacity and patient access and are contributing to hospitals' profits, several critiques of the research have been presented in the literature.

A third area of study seeks to quantify the role of hospitals as centers of economic activity—hubs of employment, payers of wages, purchasers of goods and services, and generators of tax revenue. Freeman, Sidhu, and Montoya (2006) note that Los Angeles County–area hospitals were directly or indirectly responsible for generating over $47 billion in revenue in 2004, including direct revenue attributed to hospitals and the hospital-related portion of revenues from doctors' offices and medical labs, and indirect revenue generated when hospitals, doctors' offices, labs, and their employees buy goods and services in the local area.

Although the focuses of the studies have varied, their conclusions are the same—hospitals are major economic drivers of their respective communities. But two key elements are lacking from the existing research. First, the studies lack a more detailed examination of a hospital's community. In particular, when we explore hospitals through a statewide, regional, or county lens, we miss the impact of the hospital on its surrounding community. Second, previous studies have treated all hospitals equally and have not systematically taken into account the size of the particular facilities. As a result, the economic impacts of small, medium, and large hospitals have been collapsed together. We addressed both issues in selecting the hospitals for our study.

We are particularly interested in the interaction between neighborhood characteristics (race or ethnicity and income) and the presence of a hospital. Does agglomeration of health care businesses occur equally over all places, or is it affected by neighborhood characteristics? Put another way, we seek evidence on whether hospitals are an engine for economic development in consistent ways, or whether a hospital's effect is influenced by social, demographic, and political factors apart from pure economics. Through these questions we hope to uncover the role of the hospital as a large landowner within the local real estate market.

Studying Hospitals: Taking a Neighborhood Census

Our research approach involves conducting a visual census of land uses for parcels located close to the hospital. The objective is to establish the full range of activities taking place around hospitals and then to infer the links between hospitals and their environs. A second objective is to establish the extent to which hospitals anchor agglomerations of health-related activities. Thus, beyond classifying parcels according to broad land use, the census also identifies the type of activity taking place on parcels with health-related activities. This information can provide an indication of the nature of clustering of activities, an important feature of agglomeration economies. A third goal is to establish whether these relationships differ across hospitals located in different types of neighborhoods. This question highlights important distributional issues regarding the benefits hospitals confer on the neighborhoods and populations with which they interact.

Although it is quite labor intensive, the visual parcel-level census approach is appropriate for this research for several reasons. First, almost no dataset provides reliable information on land uses at the parcel level. This is because collecting such information is expensive, and because, even if data are collected, uses can change and these changes can go unnoticed for some time by those collecting the information. Second, individual parcels might feature multiple land uses. For example, parcels may feature housing with retail stores or gas stations and convenience stores. A visual census permits the accurate identification of these mixed uses. Third, the census allows for the identification of business activities that might not be recorded in the phone book or other potential source of information. A dentist, accountant, or massage therapist might have a small operation run out of a home or other nontraditional business location. Although it does not eliminate these issues altogether, the parcel-level census approach increases coverage and accuracy and reduces the likelihood that important land uses will be overlooked.

A key issue is how to define a hospital's "neighborhood." We use a one-mile radius around a hospital as the boundary of its neighborhood. This represents a compromise: in some cases this radius will be too large, and in others it will not be large enough. However, given the lack of a consensus view in the literature, the choice of a one-mile radius served to ensure project tractability.

The study focuses on Los Angeles County, which lies at the core of a large, dynamic, and demographically diverse metropolitan area. The second-largest city in the United States and a gateway city that draws population from origins worldwide, Los Angeles is highly varied and thus offers a natural laboratory for evaluating the relationship between hospitals and their surrounding neighborhoods and whether these relationships vary with the hospital's neighborhood.

In terms of health economies, Los Angeles represents an important market. DeVol and others (2003) rank Los Angeles as the fifth-largest metropolitan health care economy in the nation and note that health care employment in Los Angeles dramatically outpaced overall employment between 1980 and 2001, suggesting that although health care has consistently been an important part of the economy, it is steadily growing even more important. The authors, however, provide little sense of the impact of the health economy on local or regional growth or on real estate markets. Thus, our study provides an opportunity to advance our understanding of the region's economy, its potential for growth, and neighborhood and land market dynamics.

We started by stratifying the 124 hospitals in Los Angeles County, using neighborhood characteristics such as income, poverty levels, and racial and ethnic makeup, as well as the scope of services provided. The hospitals range from full-service hospitals with large-scale surgical, orthopedic, and other inpatient services to smaller community hospitals with limited services.

Of the twenty-four hospitals that were randomly selected in the first screen, seven were selected for the more detailed parcel-level land use census because of their distribution along the three selection dimensions. Spatially, they are distributed widely across Los Angeles County

Table 3.1   Distribution of the census hospitals across the selection criteria

	Service Planning Area (SPA)	Income	Race
City of Angels—Ingleside	Southeast	Lower	High Asian
Elastar	Southeast	Lower	High black and Hispanic
Glendale	Northeast	Lower	High black and Hispanic
Kaiser Sunset	West	Lower	No dominant race
Lakewood	Southeast	High	High black and Hispanic
Lancaster	Northeast	Lower	No dominant race
Van Nuys	Northeast	Moderate	No dominant race

Note: Region is defined using boundaries established via the SPA classification.

and serve diverse communities from racial and income perspectives (see table 3.1).

Brief profiles of the hospitals in the census sample, grouped by their size, follow.

Small Hospitals—Fewer Than 100 Beds

- City of Angels Medical Center–Ingleside Campus
  City of Angels Medical Center–Ingleside Campus is one of the oldest licensed psychiatric hospitals in California. Founded in 1918, Ingleside is a 70-bed acute psychiatric hospital and full-service mental health center. The campus sits on five acres near the San Gabriel Mountains in the city of Rosemead.
- Hollywood Community Hospital of Van Nuys
  The Hollywood Community Hospital of Van Nuys in the San Fernando Valley is nestled under the umbrella of Hollywood Community Hospital. The Van Nuys facility is a 59-bed acute psychiatric hospital.

Medium Hospitals—100 to 300 Beds

- Elastar Community Hospital
  Roughly 80 years old, Elastar in East Los Angeles was a financially troubled 110-bed general acute hospital serving as the principal care destination for Hispanic immigrants when it was ordered to close its doors in August 2004. The hospital was more than $10 million in debt, and it couldn't afford to pay its roughly 400 workers.

- Lancaster Community Hospital
  Located in Antelope Valley, north of central Los Angeles, Lancaster Community Hospital is a 117-bed general acute hospital owned and operated by a subsidiary of Universal Health Services, Inc., one of the largest hospital management companies. In 2004 the hospital reported just under 6,000 admissions and roughly 33,000 outpatient visits.
- Lakewood Regional Medical Center
  Lakewood Regional Medical Center was built in 1972 and is a 161-bed hospital with 143 general acute beds and 18 psychiatric beds. The facility is part of Tenet California. In 2004 the facility reported over 10,000 admissions and almost 67,000 outpatient visits.

Large Hospitals—More Than 300 Beds

- Glendale Memorial Hospital
  Glendale Memorial Hospital opened in 1926 as Physicians and Surgeons Hospital. Originally providing just 47 beds, the hospital is now a 334-bed facility (255 general acute care beds, 49 psychiatric beds, and 30 long-term care beds) that occupies more than three city blocks. The hospital is part of the Catholic Healthcare West system.
- Kaiser Foundation Hospital–Sunset
  The Kaiser Foundation Hospital on Sunset Boulevard is a 439-bed facility and is part of the Kaiser Permanente Health Plan, which was founded in 1945. In 2004 the hospital reported roughly 22,000 admissions and over 79,000 outpatient visits, which makes it one of the most used facilities in the Kaiser Southern California group of hospitals.

Coding the Land Uses

In conducting the visual parcel-level census of the land uses in the one-mile radius surrounding each of the hospitals, we used the following codes for the parcels:

FOOD (building code 1 in maps): Restaurants and grocery stores
MED (2): Medical
RT (3): Retail

MFG (4): Manufacturing or general industrial

RES (5): Residential (single and multifamily)

COM (6): Commercial (banks, auto repair, office buildings)

GOVT (7): Government facilities (libraries, courts)

NOPRO (8): Nonprofit organizations (YMCA, cemeteries)

VACLOT (9): Vacant lots

MISC (10): Miscellaneous

MISS (0): Use undetermined

If a parcel featured a health-related land use, the type of health care activity was coded using the following scheme:

PRI (HC1 in maps): Primary care (e.g., internal medicine, immunization clinics)

SPEC (2): Nonsurgical specialists (e.g., pediatricians, women's health)

SURG (3): Surgical (surgi-centers)

CAM (4): Complementary and alternative medicine

EYE (5): Optometrists, ophthalmologists

DRUG (6): Drugstores, botanicas, pharmacies

SUP (7): Personnel and material durable goods, vendors

DENT (8): Dentists

HOSP (9): Hospitals

HOME (10): Nursing homes, skilled nursing facilities, assisted living facilities

DIAG (11): Imaging and diagnostics

REHAB (12): Rehabilitation

Using these data, we established the extent to which health-related industries cluster around hospitals and whether the clustering happens equally across hospitals located in neighborhoods with different demographics. All the land uses around each hospital were mapped using geographic information systems (GIS) software. Separate maps were created that showed all the land uses, nonresidential land uses, and both all health-related land uses and specific coded health care uses. The maps for all land uses are not shown here, since the inclusion of the residential obliterates any meaningful distinctions. The findings were also statistically analyzed, although we focus here on the mapped data.

Hospitals as an Agglomerative Force: The Evidence

General Land Use

The first level of analysis was to describe the patterns in the mapped data. From the parcel-level census one can describe the land uses around each hospital in terms of prevalence and intensity. Figure 3.3 shows the parcel census results for Kaiser Sunset. This map demonstrates the research strategy by highlighting the nature of the spatial parcel sampling boundary. The map shows the variety of land uses within the hospital's radius as well as the intermingling of land uses. Residential, health-related, retail, commercial, and other land uses are proximate to each other, and except in the case of residential land uses, there is a decided lack of spatial concentration of a single land use.

Table 3.2 reports the incidence of land uses within the one-mile radius around each hospital in terms of the percentage of parcels that were devoted to a given land use. Parcels that had multiple land uses were treated as contributing to each relevant land use category. The predominant land use everywhere is residential.

In Lancaster, a remote suburban community in northern Los Angeles County, nearly 90 percent of the parcels around the hospital were used for housing, most frequently in the form of single-family homes. The hospitals with the most intensive nonresidential uses—Glendale, Kaiser, and Van Nuys—are located closer to the metropolitan core, in areas featuring more dense populations. The larger nonresidential presence in these instances might reflect the ability of these more compact communities to support a wider range of activities, among other things.

Two sources of variation are evident in examining the maps. The first significant variation is in the prevalence of nonresidential land use across the hospitals in the sample, which was noted above. The second source of variation pertains to the relative importance of corridors in shaping the spatial layout of commercial activity. For some hospitals, such as City of Angels (see figure 3.4), Lancaster, and Kaiser Sunset, nearly all the commercial activity occurs on main street corridors. By contrast, it is distributed more widely in the areas around the Lakewood and Elastar hospitals (see figure 3.5).

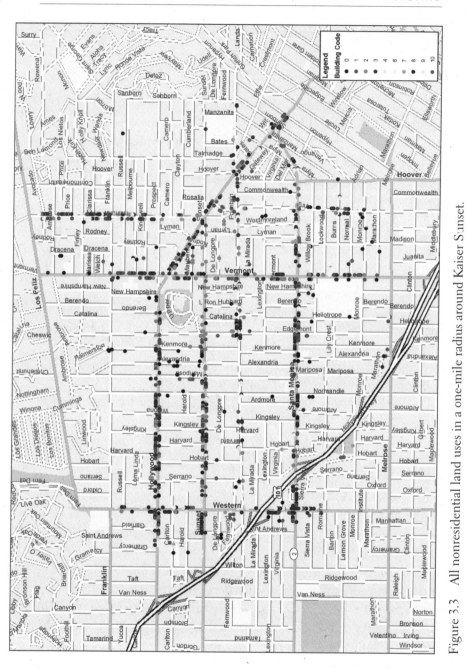

Figure 3.3   All nonresidential land uses in a one-mile radius around Kaiser Sunset.

Table 3.2   Distribution of nonresidential land use around each hospital (percentage)

	Angels	Elastar	Glendale	Kaiser	Lakewood	Lancaster	Van Nuys
Food	1.7	3.1	2.9	5.1	1.1	0.9	1.7
Medical	3.5	1.4	4.7	3.7	2.3	2.7	1.9
Retail	3.1	3.2	4.6	11.3	1.5	2.3	5.8
Manufacturing/ industrial	0.2	1.1	6.2	0.1	1.1	0.4	3.1
Commercial	3.5	5.2	6.7	3.8	2.7	3.6	7.8
Government	0.3	0.6	0.6	0.3	0.2	0.1	0.7
Nonprofit	0.6	1.9	1.6	1.9	0.7	0.7	0.7
Vacant	0.9	2.6	2.1	1.1	0.3	0.9	0.6
Miscellaneous	0.7	1.5	2.4	1.7	0.6	0.6	2.6
Missing	0.1	0.0	0.2	0.1	0.0	0.6	0.1
Total nonresidential	14.3	20.6	32.0	29.1	10.4	12.8	24.9
Residential	85.7	79.4	68.0	70.9	89.6	87.2	75.1

These differences in the distribution of commercial activity might provide some indication of the economic vitality of these neighborhoods as well as the role of the hospital as an anchor of activity. For instance, those places with less corridor development might "rely" on the hospital more than other locales since the commercial activity seems more directly connected to the hospital's presence.

We further considered whether the nonresidential land use grew in intensity with proximity to the hospital by considering whether any particular land uses are more intensively located close to the hospital. Table 3.3 shows how nonresidential land uses are distributed across parcels (1) within a half mile of the hospital; and (2) between a half mile and one mile from the hospital. Nonresidential intensity increases with proximity to the hospital in five of the seven cases. Only the Lancaster and Lakewood facilities have more intensive residential uses in close proximity. Strikingly, these two hospitals are both community hospitals located in iconic suburban places; Lakewood is a model city from the 1950s, and Lancaster, from the 1970s.

Among those hospitals with more intensive proximate nonresidential land use, Glendale hospital has the most intensive nonresidential land use in close proximity. Elastar hospital shows the greatest differential in intensity across the two areas: the frequency of nonresidential land use within a half mile is 81 percent higher than that outside the

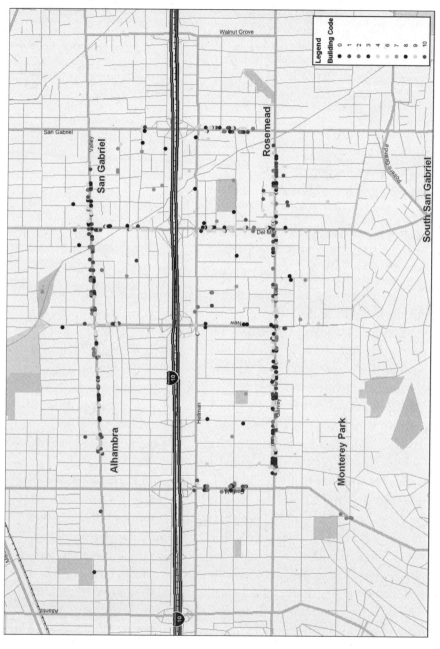

Figure 3.4   Corridor pattern of nonresidential land uses, City of Angels.

Figure 3.5   Corridor pattern showing broader commercial pattern, Elastar.

Table 3.3   Land uses by proximity to hospital (percentage)

	Total		Within half-mile		Outside half-mile		
	Non-residential	Health	Non-residential	Health	Non-residential	Health	Percentage within
City of Angels	14.3	3.5	16.6	2.8	13.9	3.6	14.0
Elastar	20.6	1.4	32.7	1.9	18.0	1.3	17.5
Glendale	32.0	4.7	45.4	13.5	30.5	3.9	9.1
Kaiser Sunset	29.1	3.7	31.6	14.6	28.7	3.6	13.9
Lancaster	12.8	2.7	1.4	0.5	14.1	3.1	14.4
Lakewood	28.1	1.9	5.1	1.1	11.1	2.5	8.9
Van Nuys	24.9	1.9	34.7	2.2	24.0	2.0	7.3

half-mile circle. City of Angels and Kaiser Sunset show the smallest within-outside differentials.

Health-Related Land Use

Because of our particular interest in how hospitals may contribute to the local economy, we pay particular attention to health-related land uses within the parcel sample area. Table 3.4 reports the distribution of activities among the health-related parcels within the sample area. Nonsurgical specialists, dentists, primary care facilities, and complementary and alternative medical service providers were the most common health-related land uses across the seven hospitals. The highly specialized imaging and diagnostic businesses, which are frequently embedded in hospitals and medical centers, were the least frequently observed.

The data indicate tremendous variation in the health services provided near hospitals, both in terms of scope and prevalence. In terms of scope, some activities are absent altogether for some hospitals but are important for others. For example, whereas there are no rehabilitation facilities within one mile of Elastar, they represent 8 percent of the parcels around Lancaster. Although nonsurgical specialists were the most common overall, their prevalence varied significantly, ranging from 40.4 percent of the health-related parcels for Lakewood to 8.3 percent for Kaiser. Similar variation is observed across several other categories, suggesting that the health care economy is not uniformly located spatially.

Table 3.4   Parcels by health-related land use around each hospital (percentage)

	Angels	Elastar	Glendale	Kaiser	Lakewood	Lancaster	Van Nuys	Average
Primary care	8.6	18.0	15.5	17.6	19.3	2.2	16.2	13.9
Nonsurgical specialist	34.2	14.0	25.2	8.3	40.4	13.5	19.0	22.1
Surgical center	6.3	2.0	2.9	1.4	3.7	6.7	1.9	3.6
Complementary/ altern. medicine	18.9	6.0	16.0	11.6	9.2	14.6	9.5	12.3
Eye care	4.5	4.0	1.5	3.2	1.8	5.6	1.0	3.1
Pharmacy	6.3	10.0	4.4	7.9	6.4	5.6	5.7	6.6
Personnel/goods	4.1	18.0	6.3	5.1	4.6	3.4	5.7	6.7
Dentist	10.8	20.0	14.6	20.8	7.3	29.2	30.5	19.0
Hospital	0.9	4.0	0.5	13.9	0.9	5.6	1.0	3.8
Nursing home	0.9	4.0	3.9	7.9	2.8	4.5	1.0	3.6
Diagnostic	1.8	0.0	6.8	1.4	0.9	1.1	4.8	2.4
Rehabilitation	2.7	0.0	2.4	0.9	2.8	7.9	3.8	2.9

The variation noted earlier regarding nonresidential land uses around hospitals holds similarly for the health-related land uses. Once again, corridors play an important role for the geography of health around hospitals. For example, nearly all the health-oriented land uses around City of Angels are on main corridors, such as Garvey, Garfield, Valley, and Del Mar avenues (see figure 3.6). Interestingly, the uses seem to be fairly evenly distributed along these corridors, with no particular affinity for them to be located close to the hospital itself. The pattern differs significantly around Kaiser Sunset (see figure 3.7), for which corridors are equally important, but health uses are clustered more heavily near the hospital.

The two exceptions to this general rule are Elastar and Van Nuys hospitals (see figures 3.8 and 3.9). Elastar is the lone hospital in the sample that does not have a strong corridor orientation. Health-related land uses are relatively dispersed, with only limited affinity to Cesar Chavez Boulevard. This weakness in influence might be tied to the poor performance of the hospital, which closed shortly after it was selected for this study.

Van Nuys Hospital, conversely, has a clear health cluster just north of the hospital at the intersection of Victory and Van Nuys boulevards. Very few health-related land uses fall outside this cluster, and when they do, these uses are also bunched to some extent. Van Nuys is the

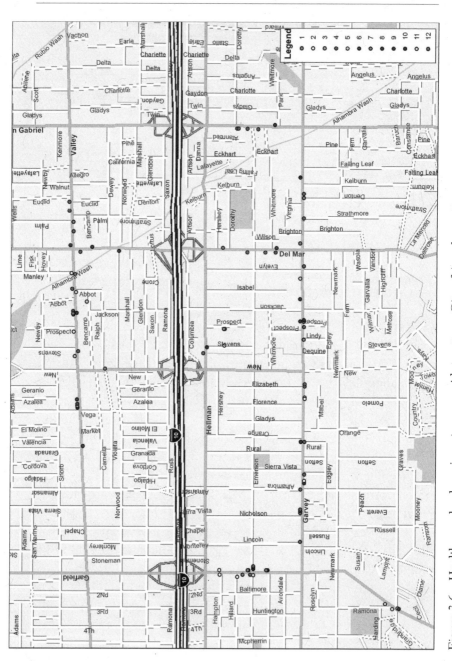

Figure 3.6   Health care land use in a strong corridor pattern, City of Angels.

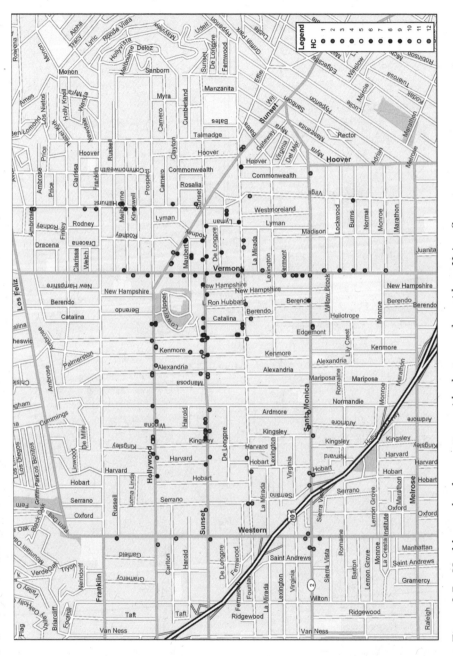

Figure 3.7   Health care land use pattern with clusters and corridors, Kaiser Sunset.

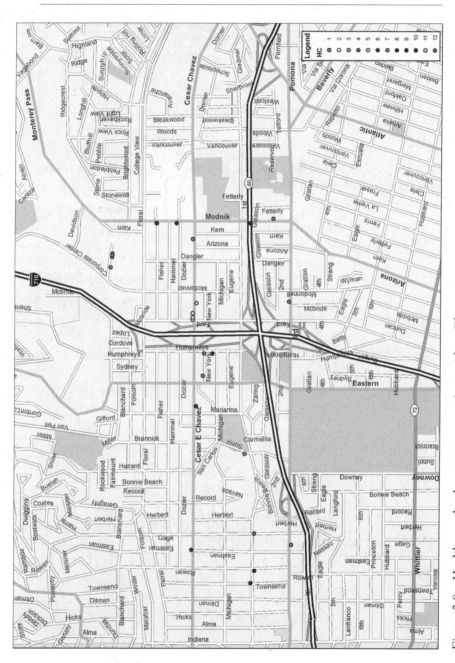

Figure 3.8   Health care land use pattern, not in corridors, Elastar.

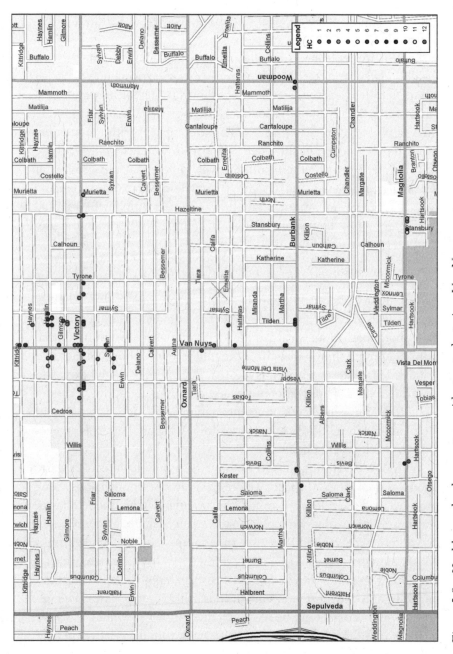

Figure 3.9   Health care land use pattern with strong clustering, Van Nuys.

only hospital for which a clear clustering is observed within the one-mile radius.

Finally, we replicated the half-mile-radius analysis with a focus on health-related land use (see table 3.3). In all cases except one (Angels), the pattern for health-related land uses mirrors that for nonresidential land uses generally. If nonresidential land uses were more (less) intensive within a half mile of the hospital as compared with the area beyond this boundary, health-related land uses were as well. Of those with greater intensity, the health-intensity differential was greater for Glendale and Kaiser and less for Elastar and Van Nuys. Glendale stands out in particular: the proportion of parcels with health-oriented land uses within the half-mile radius is 3.5 times greater than the proportion outside the radius area.

Health-Related Land Use and Neighborhood Effects

Given these general descriptive results, a key question is whether these effects are correlated with characteristics of the hospitals or their neighborhoods. In an ideal world, such correlations would not exist, since a hospital should play the same role as an economic anchor and catalyst regardless of where it is located. Realistically, we did expect to find differences. Those differences raise questions about the necessary conditions for better economic integration, and the answers might help provide insights into how to maximize a hospital's role as an economic development engine.

With only seven hospitals in the sample, a full-blown econometric model is impractical. Instead, we present crosswise comparisons showing how land use intensity varies with particular neighborhood characteristics. In particular, we report how the parcel share for nonresidential and medical-related land uses varies across hospitals ranked from lowest to highest along a given dimension. Even here, though, we caution that the small sample size means that smooth relationships are unlikely, and one must draw conclusions using "rough" bases. The following discussion should be read with this caution in mind.

Figure 3.10 shows how these land uses vary with the relative income of the hospital's surrounding neighborhood. In the figures, the lowest-income neighborhoods are leftmost. The data show no discernible pattern regarding nonresidential land use. Put another way, the degree of nonresidential land use around a hospital does not appear to vary

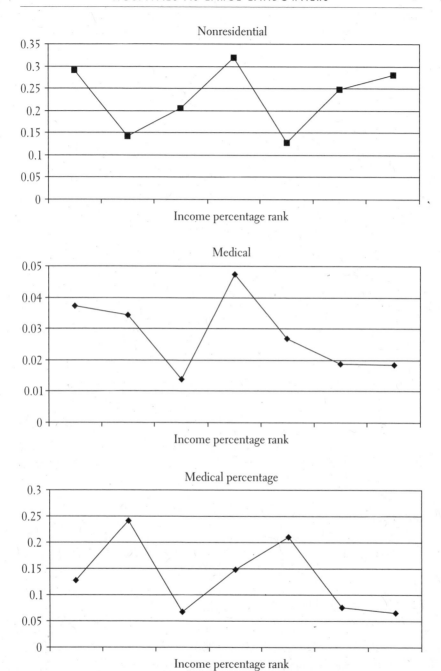

Figure 3.10   Selected land use intensities by neighborhood relative income.

systematically with the relative affluence of the hospital's neighborhood.

In contrast, the data suggest a weakly negative relationship between relative neighborhood income and the propensity for medical land uses. Although considerable variation exists between two of the middle-income neighborhoods, the general trend is downward. This suggests that hospitals located in lower-income neighborhoods are more likely to have medical land uses within their proximate area, which could be due to the success of higher-income neighborhoods in keeping such land uses away or to the greater medical needs of residents of lower-income areas.

The data (not shown) also indicate positive relationships between neighborhood income and the presence of several medical land uses. In particular, nonsurgical specialists, rehabilitation centers, and dentists were all proportionately more common as the relative income of a hospital's neighborhood increased. Lakewood Hospital proved to be an exception to this in the case of dentists: its high-income neighborhood has few dentists, possibly because of Lakewood's suburban location.

Next, analyses were conducted with a focus on the relative size of the black and Hispanic or Asian populations. The panels of figure 3.11 show patterns similar to those seen for income. No systematic relationship is found with nonresidential land uses, but a weak negative relationship appears between the presence of medical land uses and the proportion of a neighborhood's population that is black or Hispanic. If we exclude two outliers, the clear trend is for declines in the presence of health-related activities as the black and Hispanic population rises.

The data (not shown) for the specific health-related land uses in this regard suggest that this negative relationship is in part due to the lower propensities of black and Hispanic neighborhoods to have personnel and equipment vendors and complementary and alternative medicine service providers. Conversely, drug stores and pharmacies become increasingly more common as a neighborhood's black and Hispanic population increases, a somewhat surprising result.

The patterns for Asian population share, shown in figure 3.12, are quite different from those presented thus far. Nonresidential land use appears to be weakly positively correlated with Asian population share, but the positive relationship is quite strong for health-related uses, in

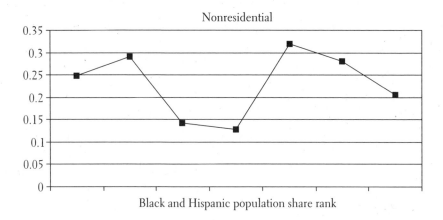

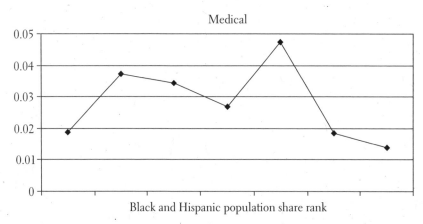

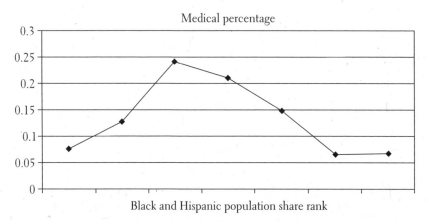

Figure 3.11   Selected land use intensities by black and Hispanic population share.

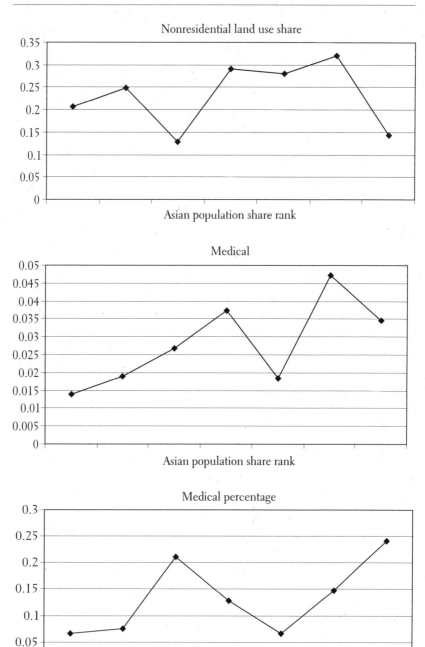

Figure 3.12   Selected land use intensities by Asian population share.

contrast to the results seen along both the income and black and Hispanic population dimensions. The positive relationship appears to be strongly driven by similar strong relationships for the presence of nonsurgical specialists, surgical centers, and complementary and alternative medicine service providers. This latter relationship is very consistent with the conventional wisdom regarding the role of such medical services for Asian communities.

Possible by-products of the strong presence of complementary and alternative medicine in these neighborhoods are the negative relationships between Asian population and primary care facilities, drug stores, and pharmacies. In this view, these latter land uses are substituted for by complementary and alternative services.

In addition, we observe a negative relationship between Asian population intensity and the relative presence of dentists. That finding reflects concerns recently raised by a study conducted through the Center for the Advancement of Underserved Children, a cooperative endeavor between the Medical College of Wisconsin and Children's Hospital of Wisconsin, that found that the fraction of Asian American children with teeth in less than excellent condition was 80 percent greater than among children in the general population, the highest disparity among surveyed minority groups (Flores and Tomany-Korman 2008).

Although the single-dimension neighborhood results provide insights regarding land uses, we believe that we can elicit further information by categorizing hospitals according to whether they are located in lower-income, high-minority neighborhoods and comparing the land use patterns (see figures 3.13–3.15). We take the average land use over all hospitals falling in a given category. In categorizing hospitals, we considered a neighborhood "high minority" if more than 30 percent of its population is of a particular ethnic or racial minority. As above, we do separate runs for Asians, and blacks and Hispanics.

We start with a comparison of land use patterns around hospitals located in lower-income neighborhoods with Asian communities (see figure 3.13). City of Angels Medical Center is the only hospital located in a lower-income Asian community as defined. Our low-income Asian community has a far lower nonresidential land use intensity, yet the medical presence in that nonresidential land use greatly exceeds the medical presence for the other hospital neighborhoods

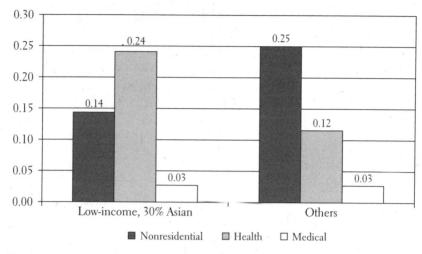

Figure 3.13   Land use intensity by relative income and high Asian population.

(24 percent versus 12 percent). Clearly, low-income Asian households see proportionally more health-related service providers than do households in other communities given their access to local nonresidential land uses.

Figure 3.14 shows the comparison between land use patterns around hospitals located in lower-income neighborhoods with a black and Hispanic population of at least 30 percent (Elastar and Glendale hospitals) and the others in the sample. The comparison is strikingly different from that for the Asian community. Here, nonresidential land use is more common in the lower-income black and Hispanic neighborhoods than elsewhere (26 percent of parcels versus 22 percent), a finding consistent with other research showing that lower-income minorities often live in areas surrounded by commercial activities (Avery et al. 1999).

Despite a greater commercial presence, the intensity of medical-related uses is lower in the black and Hispanic neighborhoods. Medical-related land uses in the lower-income black and Hispanic neighborhoods account for only 11 percent of the commercial land use parcels, whereas they represent 14 percent of the commercial land use in the neighborhoods around the other hospitals. Thus, health-related

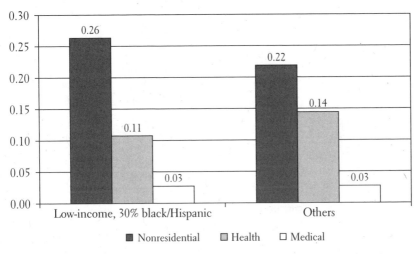

Figure 3.14   Land use intensity by relative income and 30% black and Hispanic population.

activities are underrepresented in these communities, despite the fact that these communities are more commercially oriented.

The third figure again assesses lower-income black and Hispanic neighborhoods, this time with the population threshold raised to 50 percent (see figure 3.15). Only Elastar falls in this category. In this case, the lower-income black and Hispanic community has both lower nonresidential land use intensity and, within its nonresidential land uses, relatively less health-related land use activity. Tentatively, we conclude that this case represents a community in health-related crisis. Given that Elastar closed shortly after our sample selection, the findings here strongly suggest that crisis was a prevailing condition. Elastar's closing, coupled with the land use findings shown in figure 3.14, suggests that a healthy, functioning hospital might contribute to a vibrant, stable, and healthy local economy more broadly.

In our final exercise, we grouped the hospitals according to their size, which we defined on the basis of the number of beds: small hospitals had fewer than 100 beds; medium-sized hospitals 100 to 300 beds, and large hospitals more than 300 beds. We thus have two small hospitals (City of Angels and Van Nuys), three medium-sized hospitals (Elastar, Lakewood, and Lancaster), and two large hospitals (Glendale

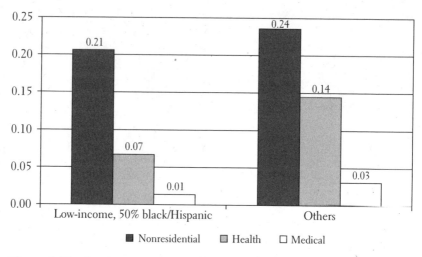

Figure 3.15   Land use intensity by relative income and 50% black and Hispanic population.

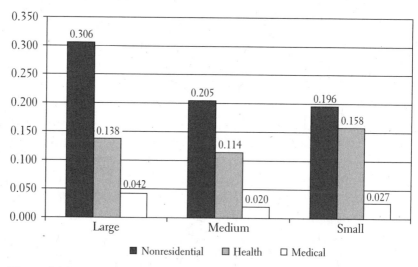

Figure 3.16   Land use intensity by size of hospital facility.

and Kaiser). The results, presented in figure 3.16, indicate that large hospitals are located in neighborhoods that have more intensive non-residential land uses relative to smaller hospitals. The comparison found relatively little difference in nonresidential intensity between medium-sized and small hospitals. Perhaps surprisingly, given a level of nonresidential land use, the greatest medical-related intensity was found among the small hospitals in the sample. We present this finding cautiously, since it represents a further division of our small sample of hospitals.

Conclusions

The purpose of this study was to analyze the contribution of hospitals to community economies by using data collected in a census of land use—with a particular focus on health-related land uses—for parcels surrounding hospitals in a stratified set of neighborhoods. We hypothesized that neighborhood differences would affect the presence of non-residential land uses and the agglomeration of health care land uses, as would the type and size of the hospital.

The results described here confirm at least part of our hypothesis. First, health care economies, as represented by the economic activity around hospitals, do differ across neighborhoods. Not surprisingly, hospitals in the urban core were surrounded by a greater percentage of nonresidential uses. Similarly, the pattern of the health-related land uses also differed across space, as great variation was found in the amounts and types of health care businesses. Some activities were simply absent in one place, particularly present in others.

Second, for most of the hospitals, nonresidential and health-related land uses increased with proximity to the hospital. This finding suggests that "land use gradients" may exist around hospitals, hospitals playing the same role that central cities or cluster nodes play in neoclassical models of urban areas (Mills 1967; Giuliano and Small 1991). If this is found to be generally true, it would imply that hospitals are an important anchor for local economies. There were two exceptions to this pattern: Lakewood and Lancaster. These two hospitals are embedded in suburban communities, where perhaps the relationship of the hospital to other nonresidential activity is affected by the style of development and explicit zoning strategies.

Third, and somewhat surprisingly, the patterns of the nonresidential and health-related land uses around each hospital fell into discernible and distinct patterns. We found a clear difference between hospitals with distinct corridor and cluster patterns. Regarding health-related land uses, only Kaiser Sunset had both a strong cluster and a strong corridor pattern, perhaps influenced by the presence of another hospital, Children's Hospital Los Angeles, nearby. Only Elastar did not have a strong corridor orientation, symptomatic, we believe, of its general weakness as an economic engine in this poor and heavily minority community. Overall, these distinctions might indicate that in the places with weak corridor development, surrounding land uses are more closely tied to the hospital than in places with strong commercial corridors.

Fourth, although the degree of nonresidential land use around a hospital did not vary with the relative affluence of a neighborhood, the health-related land uses had a weak negative relationship. Hospitals in lower-income neighborhoods are more likely to have such uses nearby, which suggests the importance of the hospital as an economic engine in these neighborhoods. However, we also found that some health-related land uses were more likely to exist in wealthier neighborhoods. Not surprisingly, these uses included nonsurgical specialists and rehabilitation centers, often more expensive medical providers that many poorer residents would not be able to afford.

Fifth, considering the relationship between race and ethnicity and health-related land uses, the patterns across the races were somewhat contradictory. On one hand, we found a weak negative relationship between the presence of health-related land uses and the proportion of the neighborhood's black and Hispanic population. On the other hand, we found a strong positive relationship between the presence of heath-related land uses and the proportion of the neighborhood's Asian population. The positive relationship was driven particularly by the presence of nonsurgical specialists, surgical centers, and complementary medical providers, even in the absence of primary care facilities and pharmacies. Though only univariate, these results are consistent with considerable evidence suggesting that neighborhood racial composition is an important factor shaping neighborhood outcomes and that disadvantage is more prevalent in black and Hispanic areas.

Sixth, we attempted to move beyond the single-dimension studies by comparing the three hospitals in low-income, high-minority communities with the other sampled hospitals in terms of the intensity of nonresidential and health-related land uses. The Asian community had a strong health-related economy that was far more intense than the remainder of the nonresidential land uses. However, the two black and Hispanic communities had a dramatically different story, exhibiting a weak health-related land use pattern. Such weakness is made particularly evident by looking at Elastar hospital, which was located in a very heavily black and Hispanic neighborhood. This hospital was surrounded by a very weak health-related economy, which was symptomatic of its larger financial problems. Elastar's closing, coupled with the other land use findings, points to a conclusion that a healthy, functioning hospital might contribute to a vibrant, stable, and healthy local economy more broadly.

Given the small sample represented in this study, these results can be viewed only as suggestive rather than definitive. However, we believe that they clearly point to the important role that hospitals play in local economies and suggest that the influence and importance of hospitals extend beyond their impact on health outcomes and into a broader economic context. Although studies have demonstrated that health-related land uses are economic engines for regional economies, we argue that a healthy hospital is not only crucial to a community's health, but also strongly related to its economic health. In light of the hospital industry's expectations that further hospital closings will occur, this broader context is extremely important, and more research is needed in this area to inform academics, industry practitioners, and policy makers.

4

BRINGING THE CAMPUS
TO THE COMMUNITY

An Examination of the Clark University
Park Partnership After Ten Years

John C. Brown and Jacqueline Geoghegan

A s large landowners in urban areas, colleges and universities have the potential to play a catalytic role in the transformation of their surrounding neighborhoods. Two-thirds of the financial heft and employment impact of educational institutions is found in inner-city areas. The higher-education "cluster" continues to be the third-fastest-growing export industry of America's inner cities (ICIC 2002). However, for much of the history of higher education in the United States, institutions of higher learning were restricted to tracts of land set aside for self-contained campuses. Their interactions with the surrounding communities were typically limited to town-and-gown conflicts about the spillover effects of students. For the one-half of colleges and universities located in center cities, the relationship between campus and community underwent a process of change starting in the 1960s. Two developments drove this process. First, the coming of age of the baby boom generation and its successors prompted a phase of rapid growth

We would like to thank Professor Rob Krueger at Worcester Polytechnic Institute for sharing his parcel-level GIS database with us, as well as Vice President Jack Foley at Clark University for his assistance with background information and photographs for the University Park Partnership. Steven Teasdale and Edita Mirkovic of the Main South Community Development Corporation provided valuable assistance securing data as well. We also thank Mahesh Ramachandran and Sarah Hastings for research assistance. The comments of participants at the "Impact of Large Landowners on Land Markets" seminar sponsored by the Lincoln Institute of Land Policy were particularly helpful.

that continues to this day. This phase of expansion in higher education coincided with the second development: a steep decline in manufacturing employment in many older urban areas of the Midwest and Northeast. For most of the period into the 1990s, firms relocated to suburban areas outside the center city and to other parts of the United States (particularly the Sunbelt). The reasons that firms relocated to the extent that they did are not well understood. Potential explanations include suburbanization, the role of climate amenities, the physical structure of older urban areas, racial conflict, and changes in the labor market (see, e.g., Glaeser 2005). Central cities were left much poorer, with decaying neighborhoods and empty factories. These changes in both campus and community altered the balance between educational institutions and their surrounding neighborhoods.

Initially, the main impact of these developments was physical expansion (Perry and Wiewel 2005). Starting in the 1960s, educational institutions approached expansion in the same way that transportation officials of the period approached building freeways. The spatial logic of the optimal configuration of the campus, not the needs of the surrounding (low-income) community, governed institutions' plans for the acquisition of decaying properties and for new construction. In a remarkable parallel with other large-scale urban projects, a phase of conflicts and then pitched battles ensued. By the 1990s, both sides were developing strategies for resolving these conflicts and accommodating community needs. The long-standing historical principle of the physical isolation of the campus had been broken.

The growth of educational institutions and the restructuring of the economies of inner cities have also prompted a rethinking of the social and economic interaction of the campus and the community. Both narrow self-interest and a broader perspective have prompted this reevaluation. Many neighborhoods surrounding urban educational institutions began to experience transition starting in the 1960s, which led to rising crime rates and physical deterioration during the 1970s and 1980s. These conditions posed obvious challenges for attracting students, and educational institutions began to pay much closer attention to the surrounding neighborhood. By the 1990s, administrators, community leaders, and the local business community also began to recognize the catalytic role that educational institutions could potentially play in the redevelopment of central city neighborhoods and economies, with the likely realization that one potential effect of these activities was on the market for housing in the surrounding neighborhoods.

With the support of the Department of Housing and Urban Development (HUD), other public agencies, and private foundations, campus-community partnerships became widespread during the 1990s (Vidal et al. 2002; HUD 2005). The Community Outreach Partnership Center Program (COPC) and related initiatives of HUD, for example, have involved over 300 institutions of higher learning over the past 10 years in partnerships featuring housing development and rehabilitation, education, job training, and capacity building. Although these efforts are widespread, research into their effectiveness has lagged behind their implementation. A series of articles in *Cityscape* in 2000 (Cox 2000) points toward some important directions for understanding these impacts, and a research report (Vidal et al. 2002) provides a comprehensive description of high-profile interactions, but neither evaluates their effectiveness. Previous reviews of the literature argue that most research is more instructive on the nuts and bolts of developing partnerships and does not provide careful case studies that could be used for comparative evaluation (Rubin 2000; ICIC 2002). The Lincoln Institute of Land Policy is very involved with these issues through its program "The City, Land, and The University"; it has published two edited volumes of case studies and analysis of university-community collaborations (Perry and Wiewel 2005; Wiewel and Knapp 2005).

The University Park Partnership of Clark University in Worcester, Massachusetts

This chapter offers a case study of a campus-community partnership conducted by Clark University in Worcester, Massachusetts: the University Park Partnership. Clark University was founded in 1887 as a graduate research university. Today, it is a liberal arts research university with nine Ph.D. programs and a population of about 2,500 undergraduate and graduate students. The university is located in the inner-city Main South neighborhood, about one mile southwest of Worcester's central business district (CBD). Up until World War II, the Main South neighborhood was a middle-class to upper-middle-class neighborhood. Areas closer to nearby factories, which were built

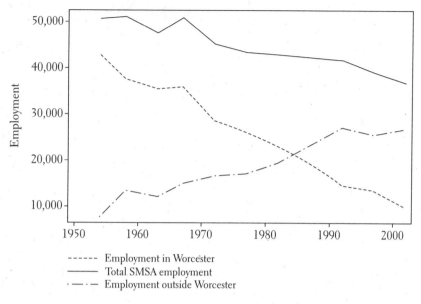

Figure 4.1a   The development of manufacturing in the Worcester SMSA: employment, 1954–2002.

around the turn of the century, provided housing for skilled workers employed in the factories; a majority of the housing stock consisted of two- and three-family homes.

Following World War II, the industrial decline of Worcester traced a path similar to that of many other New England cities. Figures 4.1a and 4.1b document the steady erosion of manufacturing employment in the central city and show the growth of employment in the remainder of the Worcester standard metropolitan statistical area (SMSA) for the period 1954–2002. By the 1970s, factory closures had become more common. These events in the city's economy had strong impacts on the Main South neighborhood surrounding Clark. By 1980, most of the neighborhood industrial sites that ringed the southeast and southwest of the neighborhood had been converted to other uses or abandoned. A familiar process of housing deterioration, tax delinquency, and outright abandonment set in. Illegal drug activity and prostitution were extensive in some parts of the neighborhood.

Census data for 1970 and 2000 confirm the extent of the transition.

Figure 4.1b   The development of manufacturing in the Worcester SMSA: value added, 1954–2002.

During that period, average family income in the Main South neighborhood around Clark University went from 83 percent to 44 percent of the city average.[1] Relative and absolute poverty increased so that by 2000, one-third of residents were below the poverty line. Home ownership rates went from one-half to one-third of the city average. By 2000, the majority of the population belonged to ethnic minorities, and about 55 percent of residents spoke a language other than English.

The strategy that Clark adopted in response to the challenges posed by this neighborhood transition recognized the key linkages between neighborhood quality and institutional success. It represents an alternative to two other approaches that have been chosen by other institutions in similar circumstances. Attempts to physically reshape the neighborhood by creating a buffer around the university, either by buying up all the property in the vicinity of the university, as other larger universities with more resources have been able to do, or building tall fences around the campus, would be impractical and inconsis-

1. The two census tracts are 7312.01 and 7313. Clark University occupies a third tract, 7312.02.

tent with the mission of the university. The university also rejected a move from the central city of Worcester, which it concluded would also be inconsistent with its historical role of serving as an educational gateway for the children of local middle- and working-class residents. The strategy that emerged from this decision emphasized engagement and investment in the Main South community. Its development followed two phases.

The university first established a partnership with local residents, businesses, and churches to stimulate and revitalize the area in the early 1980s. Along with neighborhood groups, HUD, and local foundations, Clark spearheaded the successful application for a $74,900 Seedco grant from the Ford Foundation. This effort helped buttress the recently formed Main South Community Development Corporation (MSCDC), on whose board of directors Clark holds a seat. As is typical for similar collaborations, the MSCDC and Clark focused first on neighborhood organizing and halting the spread of property abandonment. Over the next decade, the MSCDC acquired over 20 vacant or abandoned properties and renovated them with an investment of about $9.5 million. More than half these properties were subsequently sold.

In 1995 Clark University and the MSCDC formed a partnership for sustainable development of the neighborhood, which became known as the University Park Partnership (UPP). The UPP extended the scope of efforts from a primary focus on the physical condition of the neighborhood to a broad-based strategy emphasizing the development of neighborhood amenities and the expansion of economic opportunities for neighborhood residents. The target area for this partnership is presented in figure 4.2. It includes most of the MSCDC area of interest, except the small triangle to the southwest and the area to the northeast. The partnership has received funding from a variety of federal and private sources and in 2004 was awarded the inaugural Carter Partnership Award, which is the nation's most prestigious recognition for collaborations between universities and their communities.

In the mid-1990s, the MSCDC's program of physical rehabilitation and incentives for increased home ownership by residents became more ambitious. The program targeted two particularly deteriorated areas with multimillion-dollar projects involving extensive renovation

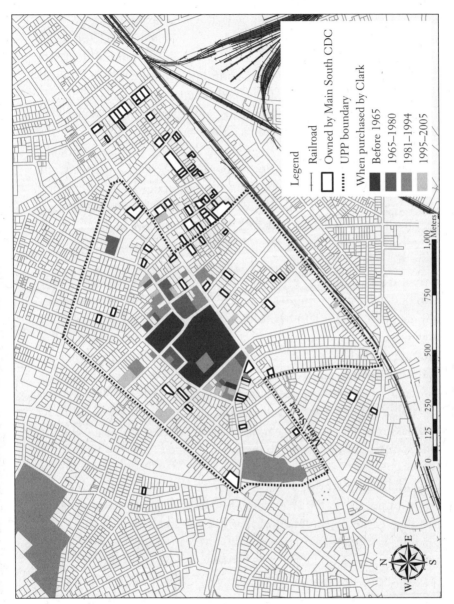

Figure 4.2   The UPP target neighborhood area.

and new construction.[2] Overall, with the conclusion of the most recent initiatives, the partnership will have renovated over 220 housing units and added an additional 80 units to the local housing stock (see figure 4.2). Clark University has contributed almost $10 million directly to this effort, and it has helped obtain another $75 million in federal, state, local, and private loans and investment (Bassett 2005). The MSCDC also offers programs for first-time home buyers, provides incentives for ensuring that multifamily dwellings remain affordable, and offers loans for home improvements and down payments. Clark also subsidizes down payments for faculty and staff who choose to purchase homes in the neighborhood. Twenty employees have taken advantage of this program. All told, the $85 million invested in the neighborhood amounts to about $7,500 per each neighborhood resident.

The partnership also expanded its scope to provide specific neighborhood amenities: improved public safety, and social and recreational programs for families. The UPP has addressed concerns about safety with the establishment of a neighborhood alert center, and it promotes efforts to ensure closer cooperation among the Worcester and Clark police and residents. For example, on weekend nights, a Worcester police officer walks the neighborhood with a Clark University police officer. Clark's police force currently includes 12 officers and has an annual budget of $1.15 million. Policing efforts should provide some spillover benefits to the neighborhood surrounding the university.

Clark has also created social and recreational programs, including a free summer camp for 125 neighborhood children. The most recent initiative is the construction of new athletic fields next to the Kilby-Gardner-Hammond project area, which lies outside the UPP target area, for $2.5 million. These fields will also be accessible to young people using the new $7.5 million Boys and Girls Club (see figure 4.2).

2. These projects are the Beacon-Oread project, which was completed in 2001, and the Kilby-Gardner-Hammond project, which is still being developed as of March 2009. This latter project has received support from both the U.S. Environmental Protection Agency in the form of $161,000 in assessment funds and a $200,000 cleanup grant, and from HUD in the form of a $1 million Brownfield Economic Development grant and a $1 million Neighborhood Improvement Program grant, to help in the remediation of abandoned brownfield sites (EPA).

Finally, since 1995, the UPP has developed programs to improve the economic well-being of its residents. These initiatives focus on assisting the development of small businesses and providing residents with enhanced opportunities for training and education. The business development efforts include the renovation of several blocks of commercial storefronts and access to small business loans. Training programs in computer skills complement the career counseling and job placement assistance offered to residents.

The most innovative feature of the education and training efforts has been the creation of a targeted partnership offering access to a high-quality education for young people living in the neighborhood. In 1997 Clark University and the Worcester Public Schools established the University Park Campus School (UPCS) for students in grades seven through twelve. The Campus School is a neighborhood school of the Worcester school system that serves about 200 students. As with other public schools, eligibility for enrollment is limited to a defined neighborhood, in this case, the UPP area of figure 4.2 plus the southwest triangle area of the MSCDC target area. Overall, the district includes a good share of the residential areas of the Main South neighborhood. The backgrounds of the students reflect the socioeconomic conditions of the neighborhood: 70 percent are eligible for the free lunch program; 60 percent do not use English as their primary language at home; and 50 percent of the students entering the seventh grade are reading at a third-grade level.

Over the nine years since its creation, the school's strong curriculum and innovative programming have earned it a reputation as one of the finest urban secondary schools in Massachusetts. Performance on standardized tests is very strong: students score in the top 10 percent of all schools—both urban and suburban—in the state. All graduates of the UPCS have gone on to college. The dropout rate for students at comparable Worcester public high schools is about two-thirds. Clark allows UPCS students to use Clark's library and gym, and Clark faculty and students volunteer time at the UPCS (Afshar 2005).

For high school graduates in the neighborhood, Clark University offers an unusual benefit. It is only one of a few universities in the nation to offer an unlimited number of full-tuition scholarships for neighborhood residents. Any of the approximately 10,000 residents (3,500 households) who have lived in the neighborhood for at least five years and who can also meet admissions standards are eligible. To date, 27 students from the neighborhood have received these scholarships. As figure 4.2 indicates, a small triangle of the UPCS catchment to the southwest does not receive the tuition benefit.

These initiatives have prompted an expansion in the participation of Clark and its partners in the local property market. Figure 4.2 also shows the expansion of Clark's land acquisition in Main South over the past half century, as well as the properties that have been purchased and renovated by the MSCDC. Up until the early 1970s, Clark's holdings in the area totaled about 21 acres; only a few additions had been made to the original campus on Main Street since it was acquired in the mid-1880s. Since the 1970s, the university's holdings in the immediate area have doubled. The expansion in the 1970s and early 1980s was primarily for expanded facilities and parking. Two-fifths of Clark's current holdings of 45 acres have been purchased since the mid-1980s. Some of these acquisitions have remained in private sector usage—for example, as rental housing or commercial storefronts.

Figure 4.2 also shows the properties that have been held at one time or another by Clark's partner, the MSCDC. Table 4.1 places the holdings of both partners in the effort to improve the Main South neighborhood in the context of all property holdings in Main South. Clark and its partner hold about 18 percent of the area (75 out of 406 acres). These holdings amount to about 25 percent of the valuation of the neighborhood, or about $100 million out of an assessed valuation of $408 million in the neighborhood. The $85 million invested in the neighborhood amounts to about $20 per $100 of neighborhood valuation.

Research Questions and Empirical Strategy

Since 1995, the UPP has invested several million dollars in initiatives that, by benefiting the residents of the target area, should also benefit the university. The thrust of the program is to offer concentrated educational and other benefits that are designed to enhance residential stability and to create strong incentives for educational performance. In the terms of urban economics, these efforts are designed to augment a range of neighborhood amenities and may be characterized as

Table 4.1 Clark University's property holdings in the Main South/University Park neighborhood, 2004

Landowner	Total valuation ($000s)	Total number of parcels	Total area in acres	Valuation as percentage of total	No. of parcels as percentage of total	Area as percentage of total
Clark University	87,913	78	45.4	21.6	4.8	11.2
Main South Partners of Clark						
Main South Development Corporation	2,908	35	5.4	0.7	2.1	1.3
Beacon-Oread partnership	2,032	9	2.3	0.5	0.5	0.6
Kilby-Gardner-Hammond partnership	1,153	15	7.2	0.3	0.9	1.8
City of Worcester	10,736	19	20.4	2.6	1.1	5.0
All others	302,974	1,497	324.9	74.3	90.5	80.1
Total	407,716	1,653	405.7			

Sources: Assessment data for the city of Worcester, 2004, and Clark University (personal communication).

Note: Main South Partners includes the Main South Development Corporation, the Beacon-Oread partnership, and the Kilby-Gardner-Hammond partnership. The two partnerships are redevelopment efforts involving both renovation and new construction, the construction of a new Boys and Girls Club facility, and the development of new athletic fields.

a *neighborhood good*: a good generally available to all residents of a few or several city blocks of a city.[3]

Several approaches have been taken in the literature to assess the success of efforts to provide neighborhood goods. Two of the measures frequently used are patterns of turnover of property and changes in home ownership. Both of these indicators are of interest and are reviewed here. The economic theory of the determination of land rents (and value) suggests a more comprehensive measure. Provided that some mechanism such as travel costs or limits on eligibility restricts access to the enjoyment of neighborhood goods, competitive land (and housing) markets in urban areas should lead to the capitalization of neighborhood goods in the value of (residential) property. Capitalization occurs because renters (or purchasers) of housing with similar preferences and levels of wealth should also derive an equal degree of well-being wherever they locate in the urban area.

In a reasonably transparent and efficient housing market, bidding among potential residents of any urban area for scarce housing creates site-specific premiums (or discounts) for features of property that are not elastically supplied. The premiums ensure equalization of well-being for similar residents.[4] These premiums provide lower-bound (or upper-bound) estimates of how much residents of the city value a site-specific feature.[5] In the case of the UPP, we would expect the amenities provided only to residents of the area to generate a market premium for housing in the area.

Our research strategy proceeds in two steps. We first investigate the general movement in property prices in the UPP neighborhood compared with changes in property prices in the Worcester and metropoli-

---

3. Fujita (1989, ch. 6) provides both a precise definition and an overview of the neighborhood goods phenomenon.

4. This will not necessarily be true if wages also capture some of the localized amenities, but that seems improbable for workers in such a small subarea of the Worcester labor market.

5. If the bid of a household with a given level of utility u and consumption of all other goods X for an amenity of level A is $\phi(u, X, A)$, then the rent $R(A)$ actually paid for the amenity will be equal to or less than ϕ, which in turn must have been greater than all other bids $\phi' < \phi$. Households receiving greater utility from A (given the same level of other consumption, X) will in turn offer a higher bid. In any event, their valuation could be significantly higher than the price actually paid. Note as well that among households with similar income and resources, those with stronger preferences for the education, safety, and recreational benefits of the UPP would be likely to outbid others. This implication of the capitalization hypothesis will be explored in subsequent research.

tan Worcester markets. If the capitalization hypothesis is true, we would expect similar properties in the UPP neighborhood to have appreciated (particularly after the mid-1990s). Our investigation of this hypothesis uses repeat sales indexes of prices for the period 1988–2005. The results of this investigation suggest some support for the hypothesis, but we preferred to apply a more fine-grained approach as a follow-up.

The unique spatial features of the UPP lend themselves to an application of an alternative hedonic approach.[6] Here we draw on one unique spatial feature of the UPP: access to some key features of the UPP is spatially restricted. The clear demarcation of a boundary running through otherwise similar subdistricts of the Main South neighborhood will help us test the hypothesis that the neighborhood amenities provided by the UPP have been capitalized in housing values.

Empirical Models and Specification

Any effort to infer changes in location-specific amenities from data derived from housing markets poses the challenge of controlling for the heterogeneity of housing. If unmeasured characteristics of housing are correlated with the local amenity of interest, estimates of the amenity's impact on housing (and land) values will overstate the true impact of the amenity. One approach to addressing this problem of unmeasured heterogeneity is to use data on repeat sales of housing if there are significant changes in the amenity over time. Known as the *weighted repeat sales* (WRS) method, the index is estimated from the following equation:

$$\ln(P_{it}) - \ln(P_{i\tau}) = \alpha + \sum_{t=1}^{T} \gamma_t D_{it} + \varepsilon_{it} \tag{1}$$

where P_{it} is the price of house i at the time of sale, $P_{i\tau}$ is the price of the same house at the time of the prior sale, and D_{it} takes on the value of -1 at the time of the prior sale and 1 at the time of the sale. The error term ε_{it} is assumed to be independently and identically distributed. The vector of coefficients γ_t resulting from estimating this equation is an estimate of the quarterly or annual change in the index of prices

6. See Cheshire and Sheppard (1995) for an illustration of this approach, which successfully identifies separate influences on land rents using information on housing prices.

in year t relative to the base year α.[7] Recent applications of the repeat sales methodology have included explicit measures for time-variant changes in disamenities, such as pollution or crime (Zabel 1999; Schwartz, Susin, and Voicu 2003). Provided that there have not been substantial changes in housing characteristics, the repeat sales methodology should capture changes in influences on housing prices that are not associated with an individual sale.

The drawbacks of the repeat sales methodology are well known (Case and Shiller 1987). One concern is that the error term may not be strictly independent and identically distributed; changes in housing prices may be positively related to the elapsed time between sales as the quality of the home drifts from what prevailed at the time of the initial sale. Case and Shiller (1987, 15) argue that this implies that the variance of the error term will be greater with more time between sales. They propose a generalized least-squares procedure that weights each observation of a pair of sales with an estimated standard error that reflects the length of time between sales. The repeat sales indexes estimated here use this procedure.[8]

We first estimate a quarterly repeat sales index for two submarkets of the Worcester housing market—single-family homes and two- and three-family homes—to establish a base-level estimate of the movement in housing prices in the Worcester market. We then test the capitalization hypothesis that there were differences between price movements in the entire Worcester housing market and the UPP neighborhood. This estimated equation is

$$\ln(P_{it}) - \ln(P_{i\tau}) = \alpha + \sum_{t=1}^{T} \gamma_t D_{it} + \delta_0 Z_{it} + \sum_{t=1}^{T} \delta_t Z_{it} D_{it} + \varepsilon_{it} \qquad (2)$$

where Z_{it} takes on the value of 1 if the property lies within the UPP neighborhood and 0 otherwise. Note that Z_{it} equals 0 until 1996, when the UPP was established. The test of the hypothesis is a test that the coefficient vector $(\delta_{1989}, \delta_{1990}, \dots \delta_{2005})$ is nonzero and individual coefficients (δ_t) are positive. Because the number of repeat sales within the

---

7. See Calhoun (1996) for a more detailed discussion of this methodology.

8. One other criticism of the repeat sales methodology argues that the sample of homes sold two or more times during a period may suffer from sample selection bias. Researchers have argued that indexes covering a long enough time series of sales may mitigate this potential problem.

UPP neighborhood does not support the estimation of a quarterly index, we estimate an annual version of a repeat sales index.

The alternative hedonic approach has the advantage of using all the information on property sales in a market rather than just repeat sales. In addition, the influence of some particular features of the housing or local amenities (or disamenities) may be of interest. Rosen (1974) provides the theoretical underpinnings of the hedonic model and the theory of implicit markets. In the context of housing and property markets, hedonic theory suggests that the market price of housing (P) is a function of z bundled structural, site-specific, and neighborhood characteristics ($P(z)$) and is equal to the purchaser's bid. The theory of implicit markets asserts that the purchaser's bid is in turn a function of how much the purchaser values the characteristics, each of which is traded in an implicit market. To get the most for his or her money, each buyer will equate the marginal cost of acquiring the characteristic on the market (the slight addition to the purchase price with a small increase in the area of the home, for example) with his or her additional willingness to pay for it. In brief, data on prices in markets for housing can be used to reveal information about how much households actually value (at the margin) various features of housing.

Hedonic statistical models are thus identified on both the buyer's and the seller's side of the market. Information from sales prices alone is sufficient to estimate a hedonic function of the form

$$P_{it} = f(\alpha, s, \beta, h, \gamma, g, \tau, \varepsilon_{it}) \tag{3}$$

where

P_{it} = the price of a house i sold in year t,
s = a vector of k parcel or structure characteristics,
h = a vector of l neighborhood characteristics,
g = a vector of m spatial and location variables,
$\alpha, \beta, \gamma, \tau$ = associated parameter vectors,
ε_{it} = a random error term,

and k is the number of parcel or structural characteristics, h is the number of neighborhood and locational characteristics, and m is the number of land use characteristics. Because housing is a bundled good, it is unlikely that the functional form of equation (3) would be linear on a priori grounds. Aside from that, economic theory does not suggest the correct functional form for the empirical specification. However, previous research has demonstrated that flexible functional forms, such as the Box-Cox transformation, are superior for empirical specifications of hedonic pricing models. Use of the Box-Cox transformation with maximum likelihood estimation allows the data to choose the appropriate shape of the hedonic price function (Cropper, Deck, and McConnell 1988).

Under the Box-Cox approach, an estimated equation for housing in a neighborhood with amenities and other site-specific attributes would thus be

$$\frac{P_{it}^{\lambda}-1}{\lambda} = \alpha + \sum_{k=1}^{k} \beta_{\kappa} \frac{s_{k}^{\lambda}-1}{\lambda} + \sum_{l=1}^{l} \gamma_{l} \frac{h_{l}^{\lambda}-1}{\lambda} + \sum_{m=1}^{l} \tau_{m} \frac{g_{m}^{\lambda}-1}{\lambda} + \varepsilon_{it} \quad (4)$$

The parameter λ can take on a range of values. If λ is equal to 1, the relationship between the market price of a property and its characteristics is linear. If λ is equal to 0, the specification becomes a log-log specification. Because they could be undefined if transformed by λ, dichotomous variables are not transformed.

Of most value for this study, the estimates of $\partial \hat{P}_i / \partial s_i$ found from statistical analysis of equation (4) provide information on how households in the Worcester housing market value the structural features of property. Similar estimates of the marginal valuation of site-specific and neighborhood-specific characteristics can also be calculated from the results of the Box-Cox estimation. In addition to measurable housing characteristics, we focus on measured differences in neighborhood disamenities and characteristics of sites, including crime and proximity to brownfields. The impact of local land use amenities and disamenities has been extensively studied by economists. For example, a recent review of the literature on the value of local open space, such as parks, on residential land values (McConnell and Walls 2005) covered more than 60 articles; most empirical results suggest that these local amenities are capitalized into nearby property values. A similar review focusing on the impact of negative environmental externalities, such as brownfields, on housing prices (Boyle and Kiel 2001) also found evidence of (negative) capitalization.

Our study of the capitalization hypothesis for the UPP neighborhood exploits one feature of the program noted above: the strict geographic limit placed on key educational benefits (participation in the UPCS and free tuition to Clark University). The "boundary effect" has been used previously in investigations of the impact of school quality on housing values (Black 1999; Gibbons and Machin 2003) to estimate unobservable features of neighborhoods common to two districts that may be correlated with school performance on test scores in each district. This approach pairs all houses on either side of a boundary to estimate such a nuisance parameter.

We exploit the boundary effect in another way. Only properties in close proximity to the UPP boundary on either side were included in the estimation, since these properties most likely share local neighborhood characteristics. Measures for supra-neighborhood characteristics (crime rates and proximity to brownfields) were also included in the estimation to capture larger differences within the UPP catchment area and the surrounding neighborhoods. Finally, the UPP capitalization hypothesis has a time dimension: creation of the UPP offers a treatment effect for houses on the UPP side of the boundary that should vary with time (before and after the creation of the UPP in 1995). The final specification of the hedonic regression thus included time-varying estimates of the capitalization of the amenities offered by the UPP:

$$
\frac{P_{it}^{\lambda} - 1}{\lambda} = \alpha + \delta_0 Z_{it} + \sum_{k=1}^{k} \beta_{\kappa} \frac{s_k^{\lambda} - 1}{\lambda} + \sum_{l=1}^{l} \gamma_{\kappa} \frac{l_l^{\lambda} - 1}{\lambda}
$$

$$
+ \sum_{m=1}^{l} \tau_{\kappa} \frac{g_m^{\lambda} - 1}{\lambda} + \sum_{t=1996}^{2005} \delta_t Z_{it} - \varepsilon_{it}
$$

(5)

where Z_{it} takes on a value of 1 if the property is located within the UPP neighborhood and 0 otherwise. The specification offers a direct test of the capitalization hypothesis: the test of whether the δ_t's are individually or jointly equal to 0. Note that this specification allows for maximum flexibility for specifying the relationship between property values inside the UPP and outside it. A finding that δ_0 equals 0 would imply that the UPP neighborhood was identical to surrounding neighborhoods except for the measurable differences in structures and neighborhood disamenities and that capitalization had not occurred. The sum $\delta_0 + \delta_t$ provides an estimate of the total impact of being within the UPP neighborhood during year t. The capitalization hypothesis implies that this sum should increase over time or be positive after the creation of the UPP.

Data Description

The parcel-level GIS data for this project were made available to us from a research project based at Worcester Polytechnic Institute that linked parcel-level tax assessment data with other spatial data on roads, parks, and brownfields, along with U.S. census data at the block group level.[9] Using information from Clark University and the MSCDC, we added information to the database on the location of parcels that were eligible for the UPP or UPCS benefits, the location and date of acquisition of Clark properties, and the location and time of sale of MSCDC-renovated properties.

Housing sales data from the Warren Group were purchased for all sales that occurred in the city of Worcester over the period 1988–2005. These data include information on the location of the property, date of sale, structure type (e.g., single-, two-, or three-family house; condominium), lot size, and housing characteristics (e.g., porch, attic). These data were merged with the GIS parcel data to create the foundational database used for the analysis. The outcome of merging these data can be seen in figure 4.3, which identifies all sales of property over the period 1988–2005. Properties that sold more than once are in various shades of gray. Figure 4.3 also shows the boundary of the UPP.

Linking these sales data and attributes with their geographic location within a GIS allowed us to create a unique assortment of measures of very local spatially explicit amenities and disamenities for use in the hedonic model that are only possible to create with a GIS framework. For example, in order to control for small-scale neighborhood characteristics, we used the GIS to create a variable that indicates whether a property that sold during the period lies within 100 meters of a brownfield.[10] The expectation a priori would be that all else being equal, proximity to a brownfield site would lower the sales price of a property.

A similar variable was created to indicate whether a sales property

9. The data were collected in the fall of 2003 as part of a project funded by the Commonwealth of Massachusetts and the City of Worcester.
10. Here, brownfield was defined as an oil or hazardous material site as determined by the Massachusetts Department of Environmental Protection.

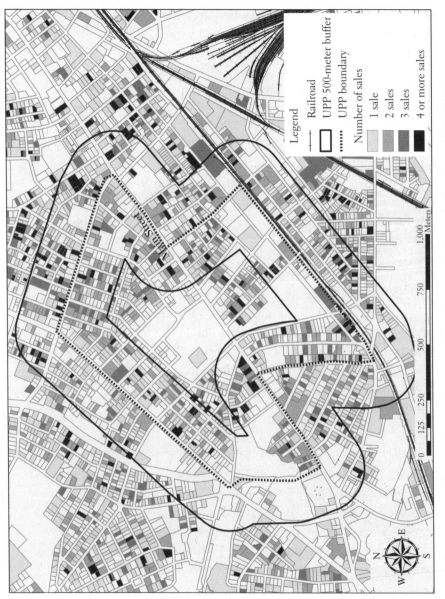

Figure 4.3   Sales of property in the UPP neighborhood and the surrounding area, 1988–2005.

was within 50 meters of a property purchased and renovated by the MSCDC.[11] Most properties purchased by the MSCDC are vacant or abandoned buildings, which, before their renovation, are likely to be local disamenities. After renovation, they should be neutral or even offer positive amenities. We expect that proximity to a property that has been renovated by the MSCDC would be capitalized in a higher sales price, all else being equal.[12]

The data on assault rates per 1,000 residents are based on the reports of the 54 police statistical areas for Worcester for all violent crimes (murder, assault, and sexual assault) committed in 2002, which were then assigned to individual census block groups. Rates were calculated on the basis of the population estimates from the 2000 census. The area included in the statistical analysis overlapped eight different police statistical areas.

We also include information on the structural characteristics of the sales property from the Warren Group data, including information on whether the property was a single-, two-, or three-family house; the existence of an attic, a porch, or outbuildings; the number of bedrooms and bathrooms; the age of the structure; the lot size; and the floor space. The lot size and floor space are measured in square feet. Summary statistics on all variables used in the model can be found in table 4.2.

Results and Discussion

We first examine evidence on changes in home ownership and property turnover. We then focus on more precise statistical tests for evidence of capitalization. Both paths of analysis reveal that the UPP had discernible impacts on the property market after its creation in 1995.

With the announcement of the UPP and the benefits associated with it, the property market in the affected area underwent some strik-

11. Steve Teasdale and Edita Mirkovic of the MSCDC generously assisted us with the creation of this variable.

12. As noted above, the renovation program of the MSCDC has been ongoing for two decades, which means that the variable for proximity to a renovated property varied by time as well as location. As an initial approximation, the variable took on a value of 1 in the year that the MSCDC acquired the property and thereafter. Adjacent property owners would recognize that MSCDC ownership implied targeted efforts to renovate and restore the property.

Table 4.2   Summary statistics of the variables used in the statistical analysis

Name and description of variable	Mean	Standard deviation
Neighborhood variables		
Price at time of sale ($)	128,260	87,455
Brownfield within 100 meters	0.07	0.26
Assault rate per 1,000 residents	30.03	10.0
Within 50 meters of a CDC property	0.05	0.21
Inside the UPP neighborhood (UPP)	0.51	0.50
UPP for sales years 1996–1998	0.08	0.28
UPP for sales years 1999–2000	0.07	0.26
UPP for sales years 2001–2002	0.08	0.27
UPP for sales years 2003–2004	0.07	0.26
UPP for sales year 2005	0.08	0.26
Structural features of the property		
Attic	0.08	0.27
Porch	0.02	0.14
Single-family house	0.15	0.35
Two-family house	0.20	0.40
Outbuildings	0.20	0.40
Age of house at time of sale (years)	105.0	19.4
Number of bathrooms	2.63	0.66
Number of bedrooms	6.60	2.26
Lot size (square feet)	6,017	2,963
Floor area (square feet)	2,918	995

Source: Warren housing sales dataset for 1988–2005.

ing changes. The most dramatic was an increase in the number of owner-occupied properties. Figure 4.4 documents the changes that took place in owner occupancy in 1996 and in subsequent years. It compares the percentage of sales of one- to three-family houses to owner-occupants in the neighborhood surrounding the UPP with the percentage inside the UPP. The comparison neighborhood includes all parcels within three kilometers (a little under two miles) of the UPP boundary. Because of data limitations, only sales of properties in 2001 and 2005 are included.[13] Despite potential biases in this method that overstate the likelihood of a sale to an owner-occupant prior

13. Figure 4.4 thus uses two subsamples of all the property sales. For the period through 2001, only properties that remained under the same ownership from the date of purchase through 2001 are included. For the period 2002–2005, only properties that remained under the same ownership from the date of purchase through 2005 are included.

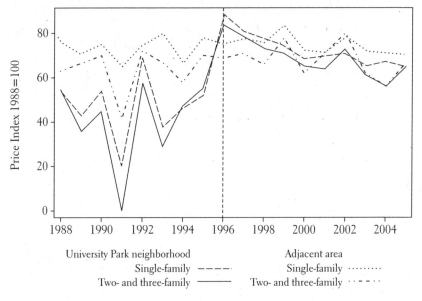

University Park neighborhood   Adjacent area
Single-family – – – –·   Single-family ·········
Two- and three-family ———   Two- and three-family ·· – ··

Figure 4.4   Sales of houses to owner-occupants in the UPP and the adjacent area.

to 2001,[14] it is apparent that 1996—the first full year of the partnership —marks a break in market behavior. The break affected ownership of single-family houses as well as two- and three-family houses. As a share of all sales, the sales to owner-occupants in the UPP area rapidly approached the level of the surrounding neighborhood.

The examination of turnover in the property market provides a more ambiguous result. One extreme of turnover is what is known as *flipping property*, which is the sale of property within a short period after purchase (see Fannie Mae 2004). Property flipping is typically viewed as a sign of instability in a housing market or submarket. Figure 4.5 illustrates the trend in property flipping for the UPP and the comparison neighborhood using the definition of *flipping* found in HUD (2003): a sale of a property within 180 days of purchase. The

14. To the extent that the length of time a property is held is positively related to owner occupancy, the figure will overstate the degree of owner occupancy in years other than 2001 and 2005. It seems unlikely that this bias could account for the striking change after 1996 in owner occupancy in the UPP zone. Because the home ownership bias in this calculation applies to both the UPP neighborhood and the comparison neighborhood, it seems unlikely that it could account for the striking convergence between the two starting in 1996.

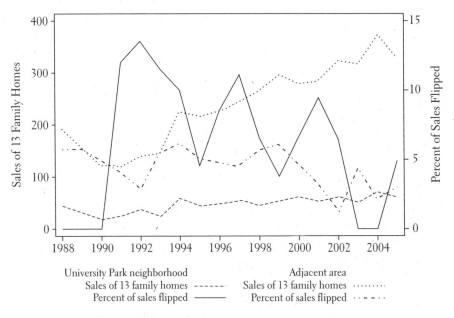

Figure 4.5   Property flipping in the UPP and the surrounding area.

smaller number of property sales within the UPP neighborhood causes some noise in the results, but the trend is clear. Both the UPP neighborhood and the comparison neighborhood experienced stabilization of property sales after 1994, which marked the nadir in property values after the run-up in real estate prices during the late 1980s.

The evidence on trends in owner occupancy and flipping points to a convergence of the UPP area with the surrounding neighborhoods of Worcester. The obvious amount of noise in both indicators for a comparatively small neighborhood such as the UPP area precludes us from concluding that there is a positive association between the UPP initiative and the stabilization of the housing market. The capitalization hypothesis permits a clearer statistical test of the impact of the UPP program.

The examination of the capitalization hypothesis proceeded in two steps. The first step was to develop a general background to the movement of property values in the Worcester market and then to test for differences in the movement of property prices between the UPP neighborhood and Worcester as a whole (equation (4)). Overall, the sales data set for the period 1988–2005 has about 32,000 sales of about

18,000 single-family, two-family, and three-family houses.[15] Repeat sales price indexes for single-family homes are available from the Office of Federal Housing Enterprise Oversight. These indexes extend back to 1980. The index for the Worcester standard metropolitan area (Worcester County) is available on a quarterly basis for single-family home sales only. Presented in figures 4.6a (for single-family homes) and 4.6b (for two- and three-family homes), the index shows a pattern familiar to all those who have studied New England property markets. The steep appreciation during the late 1980s (the period of the "Massachusetts Miracle") ended in about 1989. Prices fell about 20 percent and required almost a decade to recover to levels prevailing in 1989. Appreciation since that time has been quite steep, in line with the experience along much of the East Coast.

A similar methodology can be used with the Warren sales data set to calculate repeat sales price indexes for the city of Worcester. The estimated indexes cover single-family homes and the two- and three-family homes that make up most of the housing stock in central city neighborhoods.[16] These indexes are also presented with 95 percent confidence intervals in figures 4.6a and 4.6b. The average of both the SMSA and the city indexes was set to 100 for the period 1988–1990. Because the Warren data are available only since 1988 (at the peak of the boom), the initial true level of the index for the city may be a bit higher or lower than what is presented in figures 4.6a and 4.6b.

The comparative results are striking. Single-family house prices in the city follow the downward trend evident for the entire metropolitan area, but their recovery begins much later. By the end of 2005, prices for single-family houses were about 50 percent above the peak of the late 1980s. The prices for two- and three-family houses are more volatile. Worcester's central city neighborhoods were hit with a dramatic decline in prices on the order of 40 or 50 percent by the mid-1990s. Recovery was much slower until about 2002, when these properties

15. In total, the data set included 44,000 property sales. Of the remaining 12,000 sales of properties in the data set, about 6,000 were of condominiums. Because of their unusual status, it has been difficult up to this point to adequately match the condominium sales to the geo-referenced data set. This will be pursued in further research. In addition, there were about 1,600 sales of buildings with four or more apartments. The remaining sales were mostly of buildings for commercial and industrial uses.

16. Over half the 13,000 single-family homes and half the 5,000 two- and three-family homes in the data set had at least one repeat sale.

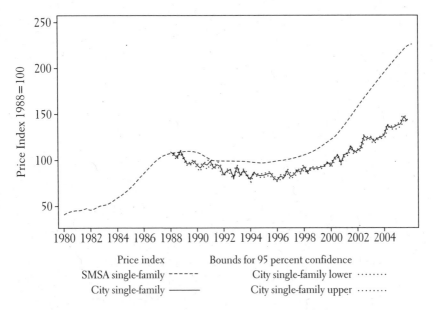

Figure 4.6a   Quarterly repeat sales index for single-family homes: Worcester SMSA and city.

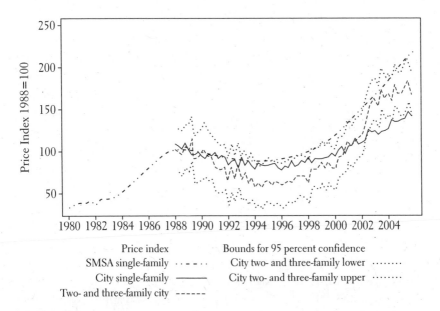

Figure 4.6b   Quarterly repeat sales index for two- and three-family homes: Worcester SMSA and city.

began to appreciate more rapidly than single-family homes. The confidence intervals suggest that greater appreciation for two- and three-family homes became clearly apparent only in 2003. By 2005, prices for this kind of housing were 75 percent above the level prevailing in 1988.

Given the background of these developments in the overall housing market, the capitalization hypothesis implies that price movements in the UPP neighborhood should have been positive after the mid-1990s and perhaps should have appreciated more rapidly since 2000. The estimation of separate indexes of repeat sales for single-family and two- and three-family houses permits a test of whether prices within the UPP neighborhood behaved differently from those in the rest of the city. The much larger number of sales of two- and three-family houses in the UPP neighborhood would lead to more precise estimates for multiple-family dwellings. The detailed results of estimating these two annual indexes using the WRS procedure are presented in table 4.3. Following the procedure outlined above in equation (2), we estimated the indexes for the UPP neighborhood using interactive terms for each year. These are found in the right-hand portion of table 4.3 for comparison (one set for single-family homes and one set for multiple-family dwellings). The t-statistics for each column of coefficients (shaded in gray) permit a test of the hypothesis that sales prices in the respective year were equal to prices in the Worcester market overall. The results are striking. With the exception of 1990, 1992, and 1996, sales prices of single-family houses in the UPP neighborhood over the 18 years of the study were about the same as in Worcester as a whole.

The potential impact of the UPP on property values is much more apparent in the final two columns of table 4.3. Even though prices of multifamily dwellings for the remainder of the 1990s were significantly lower than prices in 1988, prices in the UPP neighborhood were even lower, particularly during the period 1992–1994. The collapse of property prices after the peak of the late 1980s hit central city neighborhoods particularly hard. The coefficients for the UPP can be interpreted as the amount of depreciation or appreciation in a particular year within the UPP neighborhood relative to the city as a whole, once an initial UPP discount of 7 percent is taken into account (the coefficient on the UPP constant, or δ_o, found in column 4). The results suggest that prices for homes in the UPP neighborhood were

Table 4.3 Results of estimating annual repeat sales indexes for Worcester with interactions for the UPP neighborhood

Annual values	Single-family		Two- and three-family		UPP interaction terms	Single-family		Two- and three-family	
	Coefficient	t-statistic	Coefficient	t-statistic		Coefficient	t-statistic	Coefficient	t-statistic
Year 1989	−0.10	−4.09	0.02	0.41	UPP 1989	0.03	0.08	−0.22	−1.31
Year 1990	−0.14	−5.35	−0.04	−0.62	UPP 1990	−1.25	−1.93	−0.29	−1.44
Year 1991	−0.13	−5.12	−0.20	−3.49	UPP 1991	−0.31	−0.84	−0.28	−1.62
Year 1992	−0.22	−8.93	−0.27	−4.69	UPP 1992	−1.21	−3.29	−0.53	−2.88
Year 1993	−0.21	−9.37	−0.36	−6.72	UPP 1993	0.11	0.23	−0.50	−2.95
Year 1994	−0.25	−10.77	−0.48	−9.34	UPP 1994	−0.09	−0.39	−0.37	−2.31
Year 1995	−0.25	−10.41	−0.45	−8.63	UPP 1995	−0.37	−1.24	−0.21	−1.24
Year 1996	−0.26	−11.14	−0.46	−9.23	UPP 1996	−0.75	−2.25	0.03	0.18
Year 1997	−0.21	−9.27	−0.38	−7.46	UPP 1997	−0.40	−1.13	0.07	0.42
Year 1998	−0.17	−7.33	−0.26	−5.10	UPP 1998	−0.39	−0.87	−0.15	−0.84
Year 1999	−0.13	−5.53	−0.19	−3.78	UPP 1999	−0.03	−0.08	−0.07	−0.41
Year 2000	−0.05	−2.11	−0.06	−1.08	UPP 2000	−0.21	−0.61	−0.34	−2.08
Year 2001	0.04	1.49	0.11	2.14	UPP 2001	−0.36	−1.07	−0.01	−0.08
Year 2002	0.12	4.78	0.32	5.96	UPP 2002	−0.09	−0.2	0.05	0.28
Year 2003	0.16	6.04	0.49	8.57	UPP 2003	−0.13	−0.35	−0.09	−0.49
Year 2004	0.26	9.06	0.51	8.50	UPP 2004	−0.11	−0.25	0.15	0.77
Year 2005	0.31	10.37	0.55	8.60	UPP 2005	−0.48	−1.1	0.13	0.60
Constant	0.12	8.92	0.65	2.82	UPP constant	0.08	0.42	−0.07	−0.92
					Adjusted R^2 (N)	0.18(7,697)		0.27(3,695)	

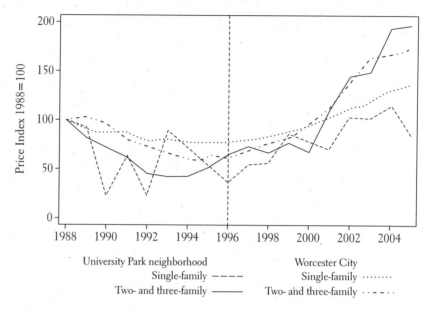

Figure 4.7   Annual repeat sales indexes for single-family homes and two-and three-family homes: Worcester city and the UPP neighborhood.

25 to 35 percent (and even 50 percent) below the depressed levels of prices in the remainder of the city during the early 1990s. After the recovery of the mid-1990s, the UPP neighborhood recovered more quickly than the rest of the city, so price increases for this kind of housing in the UPP neighborhood were not significantly different from increases in the remainder of the city by 1995.

Figure 4.7 graphs the estimates of the annual repeat sales indexes. First, it is noteworthy that prices for the small number of single-family houses in the UPP neighborhood continue to lag behind the prices for Worcester as a whole. Second, the recovery of two- and three-family housing is evident in the annual indexes for both Worcester and the UPP neighborhood. The graph clearly illustrates the relative recovery of housing in the UPP by about 1996, with the exception of a few weak years at the end of the 1990s. Housing in the UPP neighborhood shared in the price appreciation from 2000 to 2005.

The examination of the repeat sales indexes suggests that housing prices in the UPP neighborhood experienced significant catch-up appreciation after the collapse of property prices in the neighborhood in the early 1990s. One weakness of the repeat sales analysis is that it is limited to a relatively small number of properties. There were only 57 repeat sales for single-family homes and 380 for multifamily homes.[17] The other weakness of this analysis is the comparison of the UPP neighborhood with Worcester as a whole, rather than with other neighborhoods that are similar in all respects—except the recreational, safety, and educational initiatives of the UPP—to the UPP neighborhood.

For a finer-grained analysis that takes advantage of all the sales in the UPP neighborhood, we turn to hedonic analysis of the submarket for two- and three-family houses and all houses. The application of the boundary model provides a comparison between house prices within the UPP neighborhood and prices in adjacent neighborhoods. Using GIS techniques, we identified all parcels that sold within 300 meters as well as within 500 meters of the UPP target area boundary line as two separate samples for the hedonic analysis. Figure 4.3 illustrates the inner and outer boundaries of the larger sample area. The 300-meter buffer includes an area of one to one and one-half blocks on either side of the boundary. In total, the area consists of about 840 parcels of land, of which 310 include houses that were sold at least once during the study period. The 500-meter buffer includes about two blocks on either side of the boundary and about 1,350 parcels of land, 570 of which include houses that were sold during the study period. About an equal number of properties on either side of the boundary were sold during the period of the study.

As noted above, the specification of equation (5) includes three measures of local environmental amenities: proximity to a brownfield (within 100 meters), proximity to properties that were renovated by the MSCDC (within 50 meters), and the assault rate per 1,000 residents.[18] The housing characteristics include the presence of an attic, a porch, or outbuildings; the age of the house; the number of bathrooms and bedrooms; the size of the lot; and the floor area of the house. Finally, the specification of the time-varying UPP interaction terms includes

17. These sales in turn concerned only 35 single-family homes in the neighborhood and 200 two- and three-family houses.

18. This specification excluded from the analysis the properties that were actually the subject of MSCDC renovation. In addition, prices were deflated using a three-quarter moving average of the repeat sales indexes.

five variables for various periods of property sales. Because of the small number of single-family homes, the estimation includes a sample of two- and three-family houses and the full sample of all houses. In all cases, dummy variables controlled for the type of house. The base case is a three-family house. The dependent variable (the price at the time of sale) was deflated with the appropriate quarterly index of housing prices. Thus, the hedonic estimation is of real housing prices measured in terms of the values prevailing during the period 1988–1990.

The outcomes of the hedonic regressions are shown in table 4.4. The results are presented in four columns. First, the analysis used buffers on either side of the UPP boundary of 300 meters and 500 meters. These buffers are applied to a subsample of two- and three-family dwellings and the full sample.[19] The Box-Cox transformation obscures the quantitative impact of the independent variables. To clarify the true importance of the variables, we also include the estimated implicit market price for each characteristic in table 4.4. The estimated price is for the mean value of each continuous variable and for a value of 1 for the dichotomous variables.

Most of the variables capturing local amenities and structural characteristics are of the correct sign. Those that are significantly nonzero include the presence of an attic and outbuildings, the number of bedrooms, and the floor area. An additional bedroom, for example, would enhance the value of a home within either buffer by approximately $1,500 to $3,600 in terms of 1988 housing prices. Each square foot of floor area costs $6 to $7. Each attic is valued at $15,000 to $30,000.

Neighborhood characteristics and local amenities and disamenities also have a strong influence on housing prices in this analysis. The coefficient on the assault rate is the most precisely measured of all the neighborhood characteristics variables. The narrow range of −$817 to −$856 reflects the precision of the estimates. The assault rate ranges from 14 assaults per 1,000 residents in the safest area to 56 in the most dangerous area of the 500-meter buffer sample. The difference of 42 implies a discount of $32,000 (42 × $841) in the price of a two- or three-family house as one moves from the safest to the most dangerous areas in the UPP neighborhood. That is about one-quarter of the aver-

19. Likelihood ratio tests confirmed the wisdom of using the flexible Box-Cox functional form. The tests rejected the linear specification ($\lambda = 1$) and the log-log specification ($\lambda = 0$) at all conventional levels of significance.

age price of a home. The coefficient on proximity to a brownfield implies a market discount that ranges from $5,000 to $15,000, although it is not estimated with much precision. Finally, proximity to a property renovated by the MSCDC did enhance the value of a property sold during the period, but the amounts are relatively modest and are not estimated with precision.

Table 4.4 also presents the test of the capitalization hypothesis as the *t*-test on the coefficients of time-varying interaction terms that take on the value of 1 for properties located within the UPP target area during various periods. These results are striking in two dimensions. First, they confirm that for the entire period, location within the UPP neighborhood (the coefficient on "inside the UPP," which is constant for all properties) reflects the degree of deterioration in prices during the early 1990s that is evident in the results from the analysis of repeat sales. This early UPP discount ranges from $17,000 to $28,000. The impact of the UPP initiative is tested in the time-varying coefficients with the dichotomous variables for these periods: 1996–1998 (just after its inception), 1999–2001, 2001–2002, 2003–2004, and 2005. For the entire period, the interaction is positive. It also rises substantially over time. For the last three years, it is significantly different from zero. A Wald test of the joint significance of the interaction terms shows that from 1996 onward, the UPP project was significantly increasing housing prices within the area. By the end of 2005, the UPP initiative had virtually overcome the steep (relative) depreciation of the early 1990s, and prices within the UPP neighborhood were about equal to prices just outside the UPP.[20] Capitalization over time has been strongly positive.

Conclusions

This chapter examines the impact of the UPP on the transformation of the neighborhood surrounding Clark University across three dimensions of the market for housing. The establishment of the UPP apparently prompted an upsurge in home ownership. It may have coincided with an increase in the stability of ownership and reduced turnover of

20. For example, the estimated premium on a home sold in 2005 is $22,176. This premium almost offsets the UPP discount of $28,000 captured by the coefficient on "inside the UPP."

Table 4.4 Results of hedonic estimation of sales prices of properties near the UPP neighborhood boundary for two buffer sizes

Variable	Two- and three-family houses				All houses			
	300-meter buffer		500-meter buffer		300-meter buffer		500-meter buffer	
	Coefficient	Est. price ($)	Coefficient	Est. price ($)	Coefficient	Est. price ($)	Coefficient	Est. price ($)
Brownfield within 100 meters	-115.10 (1.03)	-$7,363	-472.37 (1.58)	-$15,153	-100.98 (0.84)	-$5,607	-420.42 (1.65)	-$13,282
Assault rate per 1,000 residents	-3.685 (4.90)	-841	-9.315 (5.98)	-856	-4.402 (5.28)	-839	-8.958 (6.44)	-817
Within 50 meters of a CDC property	17.71 (0.17)	1,133	136.06 (0.86)	4,365	6.37 (0.06)	354	87.42 (0.58)	2,762
Inside the UPP neighborhood (UPP)	-447.60 (4.13)	-28,634	-596.06 (3.20)	-19,120	-426.05 (3.71)	-23,658	-534.15 (3.32)	-16,875
UPP for sales years 1996–1998	141.75 (1.02)	9,068	211.32 (0.910)	6,779	108.64 (0.78)	6,033	172.13 (0.85)	5,438
UPP for sales years 1999–2000	103.09 (0.76)	6,595	-51.08 (0.22)	-1,639	86.27 (0.64)	4,791	-4.45 (0.02)	-141
UPP for sales years 2001–2002	193.92 (1.40)	12,405	203.68 (0.92)	6,534	185.01 (1.34)	10,274	172.10 (0.91)	5,437
UPP for sales years 2003–2004	354.74 (3.18)	22,693	336.65 (1.74)	10,799	362.86 (3.21)	20,150	320.94 (1.88)	10,139
UPP for sales year 2005	346.65 (2.74)	22,176	543.74 (2.58)	17,442	357.26 (2.78)	19,839	529.81 (2.88)	16,738
Attic	420.19 (3.24)	26,880	509.21 (2.61)	16,334	521.67 (3.79)	28,968	487.98 (2.98)	15,417

Variable								
Porch	98.96 (0.62)	6,330	-230.17 (0.53)	-7,383	76.46 (0.41)	4,246	-260.53 (0.68)	-8,231
Single-family					-403.31 (1.24)	-22,396	-557.65 (1.53)	-17,618
Two-family	-70.17 (0.57)	-4,489	-210.60 (1.10)	-6,756	-229.36 (1.34)	-12,736	-376.81 (1.85)	-11,905
Outbuildings	261.93 (3.62)	16,756	285.80 (1.96)	9,168	257.23 (3.37)	14,284	266.70 (2.07)	8,426
Age of house	-22.24 (1.54)	-265	-28.91 (2.53)	-229	-7.43 (0.49)	-81	-13.87 (1.25)	-58
Number of bathrooms	57.28 (0.39)	2,582	368.06 (1.66)	8,631	-180.08 (0.89)	-7,081	91.87 (0.41)	2,168
Number of bedrooms	111.39 (2.05)	3,608	73.63 (0.93)	1,311	127.88 (2.24)	3,638	80.71 (1.10)	1,446
Lot size	-0.25 (0.67)	-0.70	-0.05 (0.14)	-0.12	-0.14 (0.39)	-0.37	0.12 (0.35)	0.27
Floor area	2.03 (1.70)	7.33	2.41 (2.04)	6.91	1.99 (1.65)	6.71	2.00 (1.72)	5.75
Constant	-2,850.81		-8,017.0		-3,670.76		-7,693.81	
Likelihood ratio test (χ^2) with 18 degrees of freedom	95.1		130.0		133.1		196.2	
Estimate of lambda	0.64		0.70		0.65		0.70	
N	526		937		604		1,099	

Source: Results of Box-Cox estimation of the hedonic relationship.

Notes: Asymptotic t-statistics are in parentheses. The dependent variable is the Box-Cox transformation of the sales price of the home deflated by the quarterly repeat sales index of house values.

properties in the neighborhood. The analysis using the repeat sales price indexes and the hedonic pricing models points to a strong capitalization effect, which has been most apparent in the recent past. This may be occurring both because the longer-term positive impacts of activities are now being felt and because knowledge about the programs has become more widespread. The comparison of housing price indexes for the period 1988–2005 highlights the severe collapse in housing prices in the region during the early 1990s as well as the recent recovery. For the Main South neighborhood and similar central city neighborhoods in Worcester, the recovery of prices and the stability of the market for traditional two- and three-family houses is an important component of improving the quality of the neighborhood.

The results of the hedonic pricing model emphasize the parcel-level spatially explicit local amenities and disamenities associated with the Main South neighborhood. By focusing on property sales that border the UPP target area, we could more directly compare properties in similar neighborhoods that differ only by the treatment effect of being within the UPP target area. The results show that once other locational and structural attributes are controlled for, inclusion within the UPP target area has increased sales prices. The benefits of the UPP have been capitalized into higher property values.

The analysis of capitalization is only the beginning of an assessment of the value of the UPP initiative for both Clark University and the UPP neighborhood. One important issue is whether the change in the mix of neighborhood attributes has affected who chooses to live in the UPP neighborhood. Most residents in the neighborhood are and will continue to be renters. Census data at this point are inadequate to document whether the number of two-parent families, the average occupational qualifications of residents, and other indicators of residents' backgrounds have changed since 1996. All these indicators are also associated with household incomes. One ongoing concern of the MSCDC, residents of the neighborhood, and Clark University is maintaining the affordability of housing even as initiatives of both Clark and the MSCDC strive to improve the quality of the neighborhood. Changes in the composition of neighborhood residents and the affordability of housing both require further study.

If home ownership does become more widespread in the UPP neighborhood, some share of the benefits of capitalization will accrue

Table 4.5   Distribution of property appreciation in the UPP neighborhood, 2001–2005

Type of house	N	Median appreciation ($000s)	Mean appreciation ($000s)	Median years owned
Sales of owner-occupied houses				
Single-family	10	84	83.8	5.0
Two-family	18	131	142.2	5.3
Three-family	48	173	168.4	5.9
Sales of other houses				
Single-family	2	91	90.5	1.9
Two-family	7	84	90.9	9.9
Three-family	42	157	144.2	5.2

Source: Warren housing sales dataset and Worcester property tax assessment data for 2002.
Note: Only the first sale taking place after 2001 is included. The amount of appreciation is in nominal terms.

to residents of the neighborhood.[21] Presumably, the promise of further appreciation (or the stability of prices in the face of a general downward trend) would provide further incentives to owner-occupants to maintain their property and monitor tenant quality. Although a detailed assessment of this issue is beyond the scope of this chapter, we can ask what share of the price appreciation between 2001 and 2005 increased the wealth of owner-occupants in the UPP neighborhood. Table 4.5 provides an overview of the amount of appreciation realized as capital gains from sales during the period 2001–2005.[22] Sixty percent of the 125 sales during this period were by those listed on the property tax rolls as owner-occupants at the end of 2001. Owner-occupants of two- and three-family houses experienced greater appreciation than owners living outside the UPP neighborhood. Overall, the owner-occupants secured over $11.5 million in gains from the sale of their property. Owners of property in the UPP neighborhood who resided elsewhere in Worcester gained another $2.8 million. The remaining $4 million was spread mostly among residents of towns adjacent to Worcester.

We have explored the potential catalytic role of one large landowner in a declining urban area. Although Clark's direct investment of $10

21. We thank Raphael Bostic for raising this important policy question.
22. Only properties identified as owner occupied according to the city's 2002 property tax rolls were included in this comparison. Repeat sales of properties were thus excluded.

million in the effort was crucial, the other key components were the roles of the local community development corporation and other partners in influencing the value that hundreds of individual home buyers placed on properties in the Main South neighborhood. The initiative harnessed market forces by increasing the number of owner-occupants. These new homeowners were responding to opportunities created by the partnership, including significant educational benefits, first-time home buyer incentives, and a range of other neighborhood services not available in most low-income neighborhoods in Worcester. The result has been a significant increase in the value of the housing stock and some change in the demographic profile of the neighborhood.

THE PLANNING PROCESS

5

LARGE LANDOWNERS AS PLAN MAKERS

St. Joe and the Future of the Florida Panhandle

Timothy S. Chapin

Whereas many areas of central and southern Florida have experienced tremendous population growth and economic prosperity, other areas have experienced far fewer benefits from the state's ongoing economic boom. Florida's panhandle region, in particular, has lagged behind the state as a whole on most measures of economic development. In recent years, a consortium of local governments, economic development entities, and real estate industry representatives have begun to recast the panhandle as a place for retirees, vacation homes, and upper-middle-class visitors. As part of this process, they have attempted to rebrand the panhandle from the "Redneck Riviera" to "Florida's Great Northwest" (FGN), portraying the panhandle as "the real Florida, the old Florida," a region with pristine beaches, undeveloped waterfronts, and tremendous untapped potential as a place to invest (Florida's Great Northwest).

By far the most influential player in the emergence of the FGN brand has been the St. Joe Company, a former paper company that has emerged as one of Florida's largest and most influential real estate development entities. St. Joe is the largest private landowner in Florida and the primary catalyst behind the rebranding of the region. St. Joe has spent tens of millions of dollars on new infrastructure, has built thousands of very expensive new homes, and has invested heavily in commercial real estate ventures throughout the region. St. Joe has almost single-handedly changed the residential real estate market in the region, bringing higher-quality, higher-priced housing to a market long dominated by simple cracker houses and manufactured homes. St. Joe's massive investments in the region's transportation infrastructure, several new or remodeled health care facilities, and numerous St. Joe–government partnerships have simultaneously improved the quality of life in the region and fundamentally changed the course of the panhandle as a place to live and work.

Beyond these rebranding efforts, St. Joe has also been active in several major planning initiatives that will play a fundamental role in shaping development patterns in the panhandle in the coming decades. Generally, local plans are developed by the public sector, and landowners and developers serve primarily in the roles of "plan takers" (Kelly and Becker 2000). In the typical process, the development community has a say in the production of plans, but they are only one of a litany of voices heard during the plan-making process. In the case of St. Joe and the panhandle, St. Joe's political influence, coupled with the low planning capacity of many local governments in the region, yielded a very different planning process (Jehl 2002; Ziewitz and Wiaz 2004). As detailed in this chapter, St. Joe established itself as a "plan maker" in the region, primarily by playing a very active role in generating the form and content of comprehensive plan updates and other planning documents, and sometimes going so far as to fund and direct local plan-making processes.

The central purpose of this chapter is to investigate the interactions between a large landowner (St. Joe), the public sector (local, regional, and state governments), and other interests (nonprofit organizations and community groups) in the development and implementation of local and regional plans. Under Florida law, these plans will dictate the form and pattern of development in the coming decades. Unlike other states where comprehensive plans play primarily an advisory role, Florida has placed comprehensive planning and the planning process at the core of all local, regional, and state land use decisions (Chapin, Connerly, and Higgins 2007). As a result, St. Joe's activities as a plan maker will shape development activity on its landholdings and the landholdings of other owners, influencing development patterns in the panhandle for the foreseeable future.

Drawing from the St. Joe case study, this chapter illuminates and discusses the major planning opportunities associated with large-scale landowners. For example, St. Joe's vast landholdings have provided opportunities to protect large swaths of environmentally sensitive land, as well as sites for needed public facilities. However, large landowners also bring challenges for public sector planners, and these challenges are an important part of the St. Joe story. Although St. Joe is a pro-planning development firm, the company's deep pockets have allowed it to game the existing plan-making system. In addition, St. Joe's lobbying efforts, in concert with those of other development firms, have yielded changes to the rules governing large-scale projects, changes generally intended to speed up the development process.

In presenting the case study at the core of this chapter, I relied on a broad set of data to inform my conclusion, including interviews with local planners, environmentalists, and representatives from St. Joe.[1] In addition, I relied on data collected by students in a graduate-level planning course taught at Florida State University.[2] In recent years, reports generated from this class were completed for Bay, Franklin, Gulf, and Walton counties, each home to substantial development activity by St. Joe. The work for Franklin County has been used by state and local planning staff in support of a major comprehensive plan update for the county (Chapin 2003).

The chapter is organized as follows. In the first section, I provide a brief summary of the Florida planning context and an overview of the St. Joe Company, documenting the landholdings and development plans of Florida's largest private landowner. This is followed by a detailed discussion of St. Joe's planning activities in Franklin County and Bay County, two areas where the company has taken on a plan-maker role. In the next section, I discuss the major opportunities and challenges of working with a large landowner like St. Joe. In a concluding section, I distill the planning lessons from the St. Joe case study, providing guidance to groups working with a development-oriented large landowner.

1. I conducted interviews with representatives from St. Joe, 1000 Friends of Florida, and planning staff in areas affected by St. Joe's development plans, namely, Franklin County and Bay County.

2. Forecasting for Urban Development (URP 5261) requires students to develop a population and employment forecast for a Florida panhandle county. Student groups also generate detailed reports on local demographic and economic conditions and trends shaping the county of interest.

The Florida Planning Context

Before I detail the St. Joe case, a brief overview of the Florida planning and growth management context is required. This context is important because in many ways Florida is not a typical state: the state has mandated local comprehensive planning and established a separate review process for large-scale projects. Unlike other states' more specific and targeted approaches for managing growth, Florida's growth management legislation represents the leading attempt to implement the comprehensive planning model long advocated by the planning profession (Chapin, Connerly, and Higgins 2007).

Florida's Growth Management and Comprehensive Planning Approach

Between 1960 and 2000, Florida's population more than tripled, from roughly 5 million to almost 16 million. This massive population growth had immense impacts on local land markets, generated great stress on local and state infrastructure systems, and negatively affected many of the state's natural systems. Ultimately, increasing recognition of these impacts contributed to the passage of a set of growth management bills in 1985, collectively known as the Growth Management Act (GMA) (DeGrove 2005). This legislation called for state oversight of local planning efforts, required consistency between often disconnected local plans, and established infrastructure concurrency, a requirement that certain urban services be in place prior to the issuance of development orders (Ben-Zadok 2005). To date, Florida remains one of only a handful of states with a state-mandated system for managing growth.

The foundation of Florida's system for managing growth is the local comprehensive plan (Chapin, Connerly, and Higgins 2007). These plans are intended to address a full range of local planning issues, including land use, transportation, conservation, infrastructure, and affordable housing. Central to each local jurisdiction's plan is a future land use map (FLUM) that details the area's planned land use mix and land use densities over the lifetime of the comprehensive plan. Each jurisdiction's land development regulations, including zoning, must be consistent with the goals, objectives, and policies laid out in these documents, as well as with the FLUM. Florida's approach places local comprehensive plans at the center of all local and regional land use decisions.

Another important element of the state's growth management approach was the establishment of an oversight role for the state's Department of Community Affairs (DCA). As the state's land planning agency, the DCA is responsible for the review and approval of local comprehensive plans, as well as any amendments to these plans. In addition, the DCA is tasked with providing technical assistance to local governments as they meet the state's requirements for comprehensive planning and growth management. As a result, the DCA plays two very different, sometimes contradictory, roles: regulator and technical consultant. At times, the agency rejects proposed changes to local comprehensive plans. At other times, the agency provides technical assistance on proposed changes to these plans.

The DCA has historically struggled to establish positive working relationships with local governments, especially those in the more politically conservative panhandle. Many local panhandle governments were slow to respond to the state's comprehensive planning requirements, creating plans that were initially deemed out of compliance by the DCA. Some, such as Gulf County, were so slow to respond to the mandate that the DCA eventually had to draft significant portions of their local comprehensive plans, usually over the objections of the local governments. Even today local governments in the panhandle retain their laissez-faire attitudes toward many planning issues, which oftentimes results in greater DCA oversight than occurs in other areas of the state.

Florida's Review Process for Large-Scale Projects

On top of the 1985 GMA and its requirements for detailed, ongoing comprehensive planning, Florida has a long history with regional planning efforts. In 1972, 13 years before the GMA was enacted, the state established the Development of Regional Impact (DRI) process. The DRI process was designed to ensure state review of large, regionally significant land development projects.[3] DRI review was intended to help mitigate environmental, traffic, and other impacts of very large

3. Among the long list of projects that meet the DRI designation are airports, stadiums, shopping centers, and hospitals. The state also sets specific thresholds for residential development projects (DCA 2006).

developments that affect at least two counties in the state. Although the DRI process has undergone considerable tinkering over the years, it remains in place as a required planning process for large-scale projects.

The primary benefit of the DRI process is that all affected parties are required to be at the table to review and comment on projects that meet minimum DRI thresholds. These parties typically include the project developer(s), affected local governments, the regional planning council, the DCA, other state agencies (such as the Department of Transportation and the Department of Environmental Protection), and any interested citizens or issue groups (such as 1000 Friends of Florida). The DRI process requires the developer to submit detailed studies of the environmental and traffic impacts of the proposed project. The parties are then tasked with reviewing impact analyses and working with the developer to determine a plan for mitigating these impacts. At the end of this detailed review process, the local government is required to pass amendments to the local comprehensive plan, which are then reviewed and ultimately must be approved by the DCA. In return for completing the DRI process, the developer receives entitlements for the entire project, entitlements not subject to any further review by any level of government (unless a substantial deviation from the original development plan is to be pursued). Once the process is completed, the project is deemed "vested" and the developer has the right to build the project as established by the DRI development order.

Because of the extra layer of planning beyond that required for a typical comprehensive plan amendment, the DRI process typically takes several years to complete. A project's developers incur significant costs in preparing the required analyses. There are also costs associated with the specific mitigation projects. Discussions with industry representatives indicate that the typical DRI process requires developers to spend at least a million dollars out of pocket, in addition to the funds required to satisfy any mitigation requirements. These costs have led to substantial discontent within the development community, which in turn has led to annual lobbying efforts to hobble the DRI process, if not eliminate it entirely.

In part in response to this discontent, the state has developed alternatives to the typical DRI process that are designed to create incentives for the regional planning process. The first of these alternatives was the Florida Quality Development (FQD) process, established by the legislature in the mid-1990s. This process was intended to encourage large-scale projects that emphasize the protection of environmentally sensitive lands, design features and infrastructure investments that represent the tenets of "good planning" (mixed uses, sidewalks, buffers for wetlands, etc.), and a development mix that pays for itself (i.e., is at worst fiscally neutral). Proposed FQD projects are reviewed by the DCA, and those projects that amass enough "design points" are allowed to proceed under this alternative review process, which is administratively less onerous and less time-consuming than the typical DRI process (DCA 2006). However, only 18 FQD projects have been undertaken—a very small percentage of the DRI projects in the state (DCA 2006)—and the FQD process is generally viewed as a failed DRI alternative.

The second alternative to the DRI process is the Optional Sector Planning (OSP) process, established by the state legislature in 1998. The OSP process actually involves two separate but related processes: (1) a conceptual long-term build-out overlay plan, which establishes the broad development policies for the planning area; and (2) detailed specific area plans, which offer a finer-grained look at future land use patterns and public facility needs (DCA 2001). OSPs can be undertaken only for areas of at least 5,000 acres, which limits this process to truly large-scale, regionally significant projects. As part of the 1998 implementing legislation, the legislature asked for five OSP demonstration projects.

Several of St. Joe's projects have triggered the DRI process, including Southwood in Leon County, Pier Park in Bay County, and WaterSound in Walton County. Other projects in Franklin and Bay counties would have qualified, but they are being pursued through alternative planning processes that have been developed in response to widespread displeasure with the DRI process. As detailed below, St. Joe has actively pursued these alternative processes in the company's role as plan maker.

Not Your Ordinary Joe: The Fall and Rise of the St. Joe Company

Founded by trustees of the Alfred I. duPont Foundation, St. Joe began as the St. Joe Paper Company, a corporation whose primary interest was in developing timberland to be used as inputs for the company's paper mills. Prior to the creation of the company, Edward Ball, brother-in-law to Alfred I. duPont, had spent the better part of a decade purchasing large tracts of north Florida land at very cheap prices during the 1920s and 1930s (Ziewitz and Wiaz 2004). These purchases included miles of beachfront property, with purchases of up to a quarter-million acres at a time. Using advanced silviculture practices for the time, the St. Joe Paper Company thrived for many years, with a growing market share in the paper goods industry. However, with increased competition from overseas paper companies and the rise of the environmental movement in the United States, St. Joe Paper began to fail as a business enterprise in the closing decades of the twentieth century.

As the paper company started to decline, St. Joe's executives began the process of remaking the company into a real estate development firm.[4] Although in retrospect this evolution makes perfect sense—how could any firm with such large landholdings in Florida not be in the real estate business?—in reality this transition was a slow and sometimes painful one. Over the course of the 1980s and early 1990s, the company made its first public stock offering, began to shed some if its paper company infrastructure, and began to hire people with real estate experience and expertise.

Two events epitomize the transition of St. Joe from a paper company to a real estate company. First, in 1996 the company sold its symbolic home, a paper mill in the town of Port St. Joe. This sale effectively marked the end of St. Joe as a paper company, and the company rebranded itself (for the first time) as the St. Joe Corporation. The second major transition point was the company's purchase in 1997 of a controlling interest in the Arvida Company, at the time one of Florida's established and acclaimed development firms. Arvida had worked with the Walt Disney Company in the development of Disney's Celebration, a new town development outside Orlando. By 1997, St. Joe was established as a real estate company, with a stock listing on the New York Stock Exchange.

It is also worth noting two other projects that influenced St. Joe's evolution into a real estate firm and the company's choice of design aesthetic once it had established itself as a development entity.

4. For a more detailed accounting of St. Joe's transition from paper company to real estate firm, see Ziewitz and Wiaz (2004). Much of the material on the history of St. Joe comes from the detailed accounting of the company provided in that book.

In 1981 Robert Davis began developing Seaside,[5] an 80-acre mixed-use development located on the Gulf of Mexico in eastern Walton County. Although it was a critical hit and a darling of the new urbanist movement, most have overlooked the fact that Seaside has also been an economic success. Seaside illustrated to the St. Joe Company that high-end residential real estate projects could succeed in the central panhandle, a market typically overlooked by large residential developers. Disney's new town in central Florida, Celebration, also has shaped St. Joe's development aesthetic. This new urbanist community has received a great deal of national press because of its unique look, pedestrian-friendly design, and mix of housing types. However, although Celebration has been an economic success, the development experienced several problems related to construction, education, and image that ultimately caused Disney to distance itself from the project.[6]

Drawing from these two projects, St. Joe has established a design aesthetic based in new urbanist principles. The company's developments are typically mixed use and pedestrian friendly. Residences are usually built with very small setbacks, with porches in the front and alleys in the rear—features that are hallmarks of the new urbanist approach. St. Joe has a stated goal of community building, and it has made investments in community facilities, walking trails, and other public spaces aimed at connecting residents. In Southwood, a new town development located in Tallahassee, St. Joe employs an "art of living" director, whose job is to organize community events and promote community building. Former CEO Peter Rummell described the St. Joe design aesthetic as "placemaking" (St. Joe 2006).

The Scope of St. Joe's Landholdings

At the apex of its land ownership in the late 1990s, St. Joe controlled over a billion acres, the vast majority of which were located in the Florida panhandle. Figure 5.1 shows the location of St. Joe's holdings as of December 2005.

Figure 5.1 reveals some very telling facts about St. Joe's landhold-

5. Although most planners know of Seaside, the general public was introduced to this community in the movie *The Truman Show*.

6. Two books offer critical insider's views of Celebration: Andrew Ross, *The Celebration Chronicles: Life, Liberty, and the Pursuit of Property Value in Disney's New Town* (New York: Ballantine Books, 1999), and Douglas Frantz and Catherine Collins, *Celebration, U.S.A.: Living in Disney's Brave New Town* (New York: Henry Holt & Co., 1999).

Figure 5.1

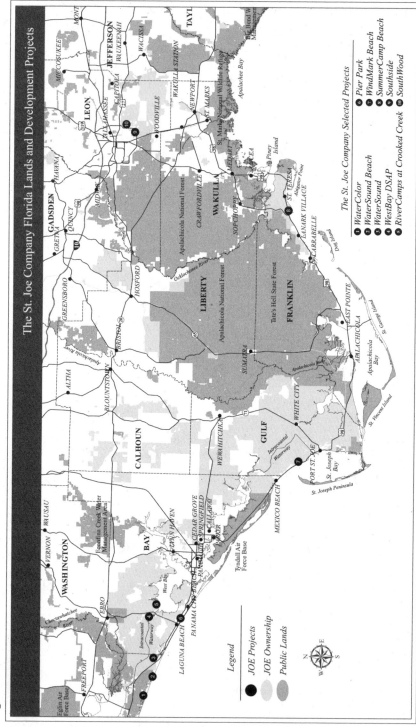

The St. Joe Company Florida Lands and Development Projects

The St. Joe Company Selected Projects

1 WaterColor
2 WaterSound Beach
3 WaterSound
4 WestBay DSAP
5 RiverCamps at Crooked Creek
6 Pier Park
7 WindMark Beach
8 SummerCamp Beach
9 Southside
10 SouthWood

Legend

● JOE Projects
  JOE Ownership
  Public Lands

ings. First, the large majority of the company's lands are not located along the Florida coast; much of St. Joe's land is not the beachfront Florida that the company advertises in its corporate materials. The company has thus articulated a strategy for either disposing of or developing a market for these inland areas. St. Joe has sold huge swaths of land—more than 50,000 acres at a time—to the State of Florida. The company has also donated large pieces of land for infrastructure projects to promote accessibility to the region (and to the company's other holdings). For example, St. Joe has offered 4,000 acres for a new airport in Bay County. To make these inland lands more attractive, the company has also articulated a "new ruralism" strategy, one that suggests that the new urbanist principles of community building and connection to place can be brought to ranchettes and farmsteads (St. Joe 2005).

Second, although St. Joe's lands are predominately inland, the company does own substantial lands within five miles of the coast. Much of the non–barrier island coast in western Bay County and eastern Walton County is owned by St. Joe, as are sizable portions of coastal Franklin and Gulf counties. The company estimates that it owns over five miles of Gulf of Mexico beachfront, property worth billions of dollars (St. Joe 2006).

Third, in certain FGN counties, St. Joe is the dominant nongovernmental landowner. For example, St. Joe owns approximately 75 percent of the privately owned land in Franklin County. In Bay and Gulf counties, the company owns roughly half the privately held land. These huge holdings allow St. Joe to dominate these real estate mar-

---

Figure 5.1 (*opposite page*)   Map of St. Joe's Florida panhandle lands and development projects. *St. Joe Company (2006). Reprinted with permission.*

This drawing is the property of The St. Joe Company. © The St. Joe Company 2008, All rights reserved. Unless otherwise provided for by contract, the contents of this drawing are confidential and shall not be transmitted to any other party except as agreed to by The St. Joe Company. It may not be copied or reproduced in any manner without the written permission of The St. Joe Company. The information shown, attached or contained herein is believed accurate but is not warranted or guaranteed, is subject to errors, omissions and changes without notice and should be independently verified. The availability and pricing of The St. Joe Company property (through any of its affiliates or subsidiaries) is also subject to change without notice. Access to this property is prohibited without the express consent of The St. Joe Company or its agent. "ST. JOE" and the "Taking Flight" design are service marks of The St. Joe Company. Void where prohibited by law. Equal Housing Opportunity.

kets and play an important, sometimes dominant, role in local planning conversations and initiatives. In the cases of Gulf and Franklin counties especially, if St. Joe isn't involved, very little development activity is possible.

St. Joe's Impacts on the Panhandle Real Estate Market

Since 1999, St. Joe has been actively developing sizable portions of its panhandle lands and has brought over 26,000 new residential units to the region. Table 5.1 summarizes St. Joe's development activity by county (as of December 2005). The company's development activity is truly regional in scope: St. Joe has projects in six of the region's counties. The largest and most extensive projects are planned for two of the most urbanized counties in the region, Bay and Leon. In addition to these entitled (approved) projects, St. Joe has plans in the pipeline for another 11,000 residential units and 1.8 million square feet of commercial space in the panhandle (St. Joe 2006).

St. Joe's development projects have had a profound impact on the panhandle real estate market. For example, housing prices in many of the region's rural counties have increased at a greater rate than housing prices in the rest of the state between 1999 and 2006, a period of stunning growth in land and home values in the state (Chapin 2007). According to local planning officials and real estate agents, these increases are attributable largely to St. Joe. This "St. Joe effect" is actually due to separate but related impacts.[7]

First, St. Joe builds a larger, higher-quality product than has been typical in these panhandle counties. These larger homes, with greater in-house and community amenities, have contributed to increasing prices. Second, St. Joe's residential sales are typically aimed at buyers from outside the region, a different, and generally wealthier, target market. Third, St. Joe has established "community building" as a development approach in the panhandle. For decades, most developers in the region built fast and built cheap, investing little in community facilities and basic infrastructure. In Franklin and Gulf counties in particular, developers often "built" (or, more correctly, installed) manufactured homes on one-acre lots with septic systems. In contrast to St. Joe, these "bubba developers," as they are known in the region, do not usually embrace the planning process. However, St. Joe's sales record

7. These insights are based in part on information obtained by my students as part of their county-level population and economic forecasting project.

Table 5.1   Summary of St. Joe development activity in the Florida panhandle, 2005

County	Acres in development	Units in development	Commercial square footage
Bay	26,302	14,475	4,570,000
Calhoun	120	10	0
Franklin	821	982	39,500
Gulf	2,422	2,523	506,663
Leon	3,743	4,820	5,449,660
Walton	2,344	3,909	833,980
Total	35,752	26,719	11,399,803

Source: St. Joe (2006).

and substantial profits have helped create a new model for real estate in the panhandle. Developers are now building housing that is similar to St. Joe's in look, style, amenities, and level of investment. A final reason for the St. Joe effect rests in the company's success in leveraging state and local government dollars for major infrastructure, public facility, and quality-of-life improvements in the region. St. Joe has backed efforts to build new schools, health care facilities, and park and recreational facilities. The rising quality of these public facilities, as well as the spread of urban services like central water and wastewater systems, is another factor in rising housing values.

However, not everyone is pleased with the rising regional economic tide related to the St. Joe effect. In particular, many longtime residents have been priced out of their homes because of rising property taxes. Although a shortage of affordable housing is a problem throughout Florida, St. Joe's development activity has brought this problem to the panhandle at a pace few anticipated. What has resulted in many panhandle counties is a "two county" syndrome in which coastal areas are upper-middle-class retirement and vacation destinations and inland areas have become the place for more modest and less expensive housing. In many panhandle counties these changes have led to substantial disagreements between newer "bourgeois" residents and longtime "cracker" residents about the future of these communities.

St. Joe: Pole or Enclave?

Given this volume's interest in investigating the role of large landowners as poles (centers of development activity) or enclaves (closed, detached development projects), a brief comment on St. Joe's orientation in this regard is in order. In some ways, the company clearly understands and embraces its role as a potential pole for development activity. St. Joe specifically advertises and designs its communities as poles for development activity. Unlike gated communities that one finds in much of the state, St. Joe's communities are open (not gated) and accessible to surrounding landholdings, with numerous entry and exit points. Further, St. Joe touts the connections of these communities to nature and the surrounding region, often promoting place as much as the product itself. In these ways, St. Joe is a large landowner that understands and respects its role as a pole for growth.

Although St. Joe may market its projects as growth poles, the location of its projects and the very narrow market are suggestive of enclave tendencies. For the most part, St. Joe's projects are true greenfield projects, disconnected physically from any existing development. Even when St. Joe owns land adjacent to existing urbanized areas, the company has chosen to develop those portions of its property far from that development. Only in the case of WaterColor in Walton County has St. Joe nestled up to an existing development, in this case the new urbanist Seaside project discussed previously. The amenity packages at these communities are also indicative of closed communities: recreational facilities and pocket parks are aimed at community residents; only rarely are general use ball fields or large playgrounds found in these communities. In addition, St. Joe has made very few overtures to the existing panhandle housing market, instead aiming much of its advertising and market research at the national market. In some ways, then, St. Joe's panhandle communities are gated communities without the gates; these are communities that are visually distinct and home to a narrow class of user.

When viewed holistically, then, St. Joe is probably best understood as a "reluctant pole," a landowner whose form and level of investment has attracted and will continue to attract development. As detailed in the previous section, St. Joe's projects have attracted copycat developers, and developable land outside of St. Joe's landholdings has become a valuable commodity. Florida's development industry and real estate investors follow very closely the activity of St. Joe; when St. Joe invests in its land, investment in nearby land is likely to follow.

Despite these agglomerative effects, St. Joe is clearly uneasy about its role as a growth pole. Much like Disney in Orlando (Fogelsong 2001), St. Joe is concerned about the type and look of development outside the "gates" of its projects. St. Joe is selling an image of communities in a natural setting, populated by people of means, and development on adjacent lands that is unattractive or at a lower price point can compromise this image. In part as a result of this desire to control lands it does not own, the company has embraced the regional planning process.

St. Joe as "Plan Maker"

As a timber company, St. Joe had traditionally remained aloof from the local comprehensive planning process, except in those cases in which development proposals might affect its landholdings. In contrast, once St. Joe transformed itself into a real estate development firm, the company's interest in and activity levels related to comprehensive planning increased significantly. St. Joe established an active strategic planning division and hired a substantial staff of planners, land use attorneys, architects, and engineers to navigate through and influence local planning processes. Although the company has been active in planning efforts throughout the region, it has been particularly active in the role of a "plan maker" in Bay and Franklin counties.

Bay County's Optional Sector Planning

Proceeding only with the blessing of St. Joe, in 1999 Bay County nominated its West Bay area for the OSP process. The West Bay is a largely undeveloped part of Bay County, representing the westernmost fifth of this fast-growing panhandle county. Almost all the land in this area is owned by St. Joe (see figure 5.1). As noted earlier, St. Joe has offered a huge amount of acreage in this area as the home for a new regional airport capable of serving large jets that could more easily bring tourists and retirees to the panhandle.

In 2002, after two years of scoping meetings with major stakeholders and meetings to inform the public—usually attended and sometimes managed by St. Joe—the DCA approved the 72,500-acre West Bay area for the OSP process. The county, the regional planning council, and St. Joe have since worked very closely together to generate a West Bay sector plan. This plan calls for the new regional airport, an industrial park, 10,000 residential units, a town center, and large conservation areas. A conceptual overlay plan for the area was approved by the

Table 5.2   West Bay OSP project attributes

Size of project	~72,500 acres
Major land uses	
Conservation	~38,000 acres
Airport	~4,000 acres
Regional employment center	~3,700 acres
Business center	~2,000 acres
Villages (residential and town centers)	~17,100 acres
Agricultural/timberland	~7,700 acres
Current land entitlements*	
Housing	6,500 units
Commercial, office, industrial space	4.4 million sq. ft.
Hotel	500 rooms
Boating facilities	2 marinas

* This represents the level of land entitlements on the property as of 2006. There is a possibility that these figures, particularly the number of residential units, will increase.

DCA in 2004. To date, two detailed specific area plans, which are detailed land use plans for portions of the area under study, have been developed and approved by the DCA. These plans were subsequently adopted as part of the Bay County comprehensive plan, and they are now in place to guide development in the West Bay area in the coming decades. The county and St. Joe have also begun work on the land development regulations needed to implement the OSP. Construction began on the new airport in 2008, with an expected completion date sometime in 2010 (see table 5.2).

All parties agree that the development of the West Bay OSP would not have occurred without the consent, ongoing support, and development interests of St. Joe. This planning effort will yield one of the largest conservation areas in the panhandle, as well as detailed plans for a vast new community in Bay County. As the primary landowner and developer, St. Joe oversaw much of the work on this planning effort, funding numerous studies of the environmental conditions on the site and backing efforts to work through the federal process for the approval of a new airport. The St. Joe community-building model is in full evidence in the plan, which calls for mixed-use, new urbanist–inspired communities. In the case of the West Bay, St. Joe was the driving force behind the planning process and the planning document created to guide development of this property. Although Bay County was an active and willing participant in the development of a West Bay sector plan, St. Joe was the central plan-making actor in this process.

The Franklin County Overlay District Effort

In contrast to fast-growing Bay County, Franklin County is a sleepy, largely rural community; it had roughly 10,000 residents in 2004. Located outside the commuting sheds of Bay County's urban communities and the city of Tallahassee in Leon County, Franklin County experienced very little population growth between 1950 and 2000. However, as St. Joe refocused its energies away from natural resources and toward land development in the 1990s, the real estate market began to view the county in a new way.

To enable its proposed development activity in the county, St. Joe collaborated with Franklin County on two plan-making efforts. At the urging of the DCA, Franklin County (with financial support from St. Joe and the DCA) hired faculty and staff at Florida State University (FSU) to update the county's comprehensive plan. In addition, the county and St. Joe undertook a second planning effort for the eastern third of Franklin County, known as the "St. James Island overlay district."[8] This effort was intended to evolve into an OSP for the St. James Island portion of the county, an area of roughly 60,000 acres of undeveloped pinelands.

The FSU team undertook a variety of environmental, population, economic, and land use analyses for the comprehensive plan update, as well as extensive consensus-building efforts in support of the St. James overlay effort. Throughout much of 2003, the FSU team held meetings with stakeholders and local residents to generate consensus for this planning effort. Representatives from St. Joe were heavily involved in all these efforts, commenting on work by the FSU team and actively engaging in community outreach efforts. Franklin County received DCA approval for major updates to the comprehensive plan after the completion of work by the FSU team. Subsequently, St. Joe received entitlements for roughly 1,000 new units in Franklin County; an additional 3,000 residential units have been proposed.

In contrast, the St. James Island overlay district never proceeded beyond the public meeting stage, despite progress in generating consen-

8. Although termed the "St. James Island" overlay, this planning region is not actually an island. This area consists of all of Franklin County to the east of the Crooked River.

sus concerning future land use patterns in the county. Interviews with Franklin County planning staff indicated that this process failed for two primary reasons. First, the OSP process proved to be too onerous for a rural county with limited resources and planning staff. Second, despite directions from the DCA to undertake this planning effort, it remained unclear whether this process would yield land entitlements for St. Joe. Because no community (including Bay County) had yet to successfully navigate through the entire process, the DCA was unable to provide clear guidance as to the form and content of the products of this process. Consequently, this planning effort died on the vine.

However, the failure to establish a St. James Island overlay district does not diminish the impact of St. Joe's plan-making ventures in Franklin County. The county now has a comprehensive plan, funded largely by St. Joe, that is in compliance with DCA standards. The plan allows more development on lands owned by St. Joe than was provided for in the previous plan. St. Joe's plan-making activities in Franklin County prodded the county to engage in planning at a level never before undertaken in the county and, not surprisingly, opened up lands to development of the type pursued by St. Joe.

Large Landowner Planning Opportunities and Challenges

The St. Joe case study is instructive when considering the planning opportunities and challenges associated with large landowners. The opportunities and challenges specifically related to St. Joe's status as a large landowner are presented and discussed in this section.

Planning Opportunities Associated with Large Landowners

Although a number of planning opportunities emerge from the St. Joe case study, several of these have much to do with factors separate from St. Joe's ownership of large tracts of land in the region. For example, many real estate agents and planners identified very strongly with St. Joe's design aesthetic and the company's commitment to a loose version of new urbanism. Similarly, some interviewees identified the better construction practices of St. Joe as a major advantage to working with this company. However, these opportunities have little to do with St. Joe's status as a large landowner. In the end, four primary planning opportunities specific to large landowners are indicated by the St. Joe case study.

OPPORTUNITY #1: LAND FOR PUBLIC FACILITIES

Almost every party interviewed for this chapter indicated that the biggest planning opportunity related to a large landowner like St. Joe was the potential for very cheap or free land for public facilities. The public sector is always in need of land for public facilities, and the ability of St. Joe to provide free or low-cost land for these improvements has made the company very popular with planners and public officials. St. Joe has donated land worth millions of dollars for parks, airports, fire stations, health centers, road rights-of-way, and public meeting facilities. In some of its new towns, St. Joe has reserved sites for schools and parks, oftentimes centrally located within these communities.

In cases such as these, the advantages of a large landowner are obvious. A developer that owns 100 acres cannot afford to give away a 40-acre site for a high school, regional park, or fire station and large retention pond. In contrast, 40 acres is a very small percentage of St. Joe's landholdings; the loss of this acreage means very little for the company's development plans. St. Joe also understands that these land donations bring benefits to its developments: well-placed schools and public parks yield increased sales prices for some of the residential lots. Further, these land donations help establish a positive working relationship with the communities that St. Joe is building in.

OPPORTUNITY #2: REGIONALLY SIGNIFICANT ENVIRONMENTAL PROTECTION

The large landholdings of St. Joe also offer great opportunities for environmental protection. As with the provision of land for public facilities, a large landowner like St. Joe is able to set aside large swaths of land for conservation because these set-asides represent only a small percentage of its holdings. Clearly, these set-asides benefit St. Joe as well, because these conservation areas yield increased land values for the company's developed lands. However, the point remains that large landowners offer opportunities for large conservation easements, opportunities that are typically unworkable and infeasible when dealing with smaller landowners.

As a prime example of this planning opportunity, the West Bay sector plan calls for much of the land immediately surrounding the bay to remain undeveloped—roughly 38,000 acres of the entire area. All parties agree that the amount of land set aside for conservation in this plan is well above what would have been possible had this land been split across a number of landowners. Only because St. Joe owns so much land in Bay County is this planned conservation easement possible.

OPPORTUNITY #3: INNOVATIONS IN REGIONAL PLANNING PROCESSES
Although the State of Florida has long required regional and state participation in the review of large, regionally significant projects through the DRI process, this process has proved to be costly and very unpopular with both developers and local governments. In a large landowner like St. Joe the state found a partner willing to work through and fine-tune the OSP process. OSP efforts in Bay County, which have proved to be successful, and in Franklin County, which were less successful, have provided very useful experiences for the DCA in working out the specifics of these new regional planning processes.

As a large landowner, St. Joe was the ideal partner for these regional planning efforts not only because it is a deep-pocketed developer with a long-term interest in the panhandle, but also because the company will be undertaking other large-scale projects in the coming years. The experience in Bay County is something that St. Joe can build on. The company has received general approval for a land use plan for the West Bay area of Bay County, and these approvals should speed along the development process once this project begins in earnest. On the public sector side, the DCA has also learned a great deal about the OSP process, and it can draw on these lessons as it works on other sector plans in the state. This successful experience should also help the DCA market the OSP as a viable and useful alternative to the DRI process.

Even the failed OSP process in Franklin County provided valuable experience and feedback for the DCA and local governments in the state. For example, the state has clarified some of the language and guidance regarding the OSP process. The DCA and St. Joe have also learned the limitations of a developer-led planning process, including perceptions that the process is dominated by the landowner and that the process is about entitling certain development rights. Although St. Joe was able to provide the technical work to support an OSP, local governments must show a willingness both to undertake this work and to manage the process. The DCA has learned that the OSP process is likely to be successful only in areas with sufficient planning resources and a general commitment to long-term regional planning. Given the

Franklin County experience, the DCA is not likely to support an OSP process in a rural, low-capacity county again.

OPPORTUNITY #4: APPROPRIATE PLANNING INPUTS AND BETTER DEVELOPMENT OUTCOMES

A final planning opportunity centers on an ability to think about and plan at a scale that planners, environmentalists, and developers believe promotes better planning inputs and improved development outcomes. At the scale of development that many of St. Joe's projects take—upward of 75,000 acres—planners and the St. Joe development team are better able to protect environmentally sensitive lands, to plan for and begin to put into place an appropriate regional transportation system, and to establish a land use pattern that yields profits to the developer while also incorporating concepts central to sustainability, desirable urban form, and overall quality of life. This approach in many ways reflects key characteristics highlighted in the regionalism literature, a literature that points to a need for planners to be engaged at the regional scale when developing plans for guiding development (see, e.g., Wheeler 2002).

The scale of St. Joe's development projects offers great opportunities for creating plans that are oriented to the long-term environmental and economic health of affected communities. Particularly enthusiastic in their support for these large-scale plans was the staff at 1000 Friends of Florida, an environmental group that has sparred with St. Joe over many of the company's proposed development projects. The 1000 Friends staff believes that these large-scale planning efforts would help overcome a long history of small-scale, nonintegrated development in the panhandle, a process that has yielded scattered development, a sometimes strange mix of land uses, and the consumption of environmentally sensitive lands. The expectation of these various groups is that if local governments and the DCA can work with St. Joe to ensure that these plans come to fruition, then attractive, efficient, and sound development can occur in an environmentally fragile part of the state.

Planning Challenges Associated with Large Landowners

Interviews also indicated that many planning challenges have arisen for those governments working with the St. Joe Company. However, many of the identified challenges do not rest in St. Joe's status as a large landowner, but rather concern St. Joe's status as a very active development firm in a region that has not experienced the same growth rates as other parts of Florida. For example, many noted St. Joe's propensity to keep silent about its long-term development plans. Similarly, some planners noted St. Joe's propensity for holding its project analyses close to the vest, disclosing this work only when required. This "closed" development model is not a function of St. Joe's large landholdings, but instead results from a very competitive Florida real estate setting, where land is scarce, land development takes time and money, and firms are constantly competing to develop and sell their projects. St. Joe is secretive in large part because the market requires it to be. In the end, three major planning challenges relating to St. Joe's status as the region's dominant private landowner were identified.

CHALLENGE #1: CO-OPTATION OF THE PLANNING PROCESS

A major challenge related to St. Joe's status as a large landholder rests in the company's ability to take over and dominate the planning process. St. Joe has embraced large-scale, long-range planning for its projects: the company projects a build-out of 20–30 years for several of its communities. St. Joe has undertaken experimental planning processes in Bay and Franklin counties with mixed success. The company employs an army of planning consultants, and St. Joe has thrown its influence and financial support behind regional planning efforts.

Beyond a commitment to successful community building, the company's support for these planning efforts is aimed in part at co-opting the planning process. The State of Florida requires a great deal of planning by local governments, and St. Joe has willingly stepped in to help local governments undertake this work. These efforts have resulted in a West Bay sector plan that will yield thousands of new residential units, and a Franklin County comprehensive plan update that will enable substantial new development in a traditionally rural county. Local planners and DCA staff express deep respect for the planning analyses that St. Joe's planning team produces and note the vast amount of work that this has taken off the plates of local and state planning staffs.

Although St. Joe understands the value of planning in creating desirable communities, the company clearly recognizes that the planning process enables its development plans to proceed. The company has become an active "plan maker," that is, a major force in the creation of these plans, and not simply a "plan taker," or a developer that works within a land use plan developed by the public sector. The company has taken on this role in small part because it is a good corporate citizen, but more significantly because this role is supportive of the company's development agenda. It is worth noting that although St. Joe espoused support for public meetings and collaborative planning, the company attended most meetings with propaganda on its projects at the ready, prepared to push the company position on issues and refute opposing points of view. In addition, St. Joe's public relations staff was always quick to address and minimize any emerging conflicts, usually by attempting to marginalize groups or viewpoints that contradicted the company's development interests. The processes surrounding the company's plan-making activities were always within the bounds of state requirements, but there was always the aura of a heavily managed plan-making process.

CHALLENGE #2: TOUCHSTONES FOR PUBLIC DEBATE

A second major challenge in working with St. Joe was the high likelihood of substantial backlash against any proposed development project, regardless of the form and quality of the project. Public meetings held in conjunction with St. Joe's projects typically generated larger crowds than had been seen for other development projects. For example, the meetings surrounding the St. James Island plan in Franklin County usually generated standing-room-only crowds, a majority of whom were vehemently opposed to any St. Joe proposal regardless of the content of the proposal.

These large, vocal crowds were a response to several interrelated factors. First, St. Joe is seen by many as the root cause for the panhandle's evolution from a rural setting, with low land costs and an economy based on natural resources, into a higher-cost land market aimed primarily at tourists and retirees. Second, St. Joe's shift in policy toward its landholdings has engendered local opposition. For decades, residents in the panhandle had come to see St. Joe as a desirable landowner—the company would allow people to hunt, fish, and recreate on its lands. Although the company would occasionally farm the trees in an area, clear-cutting hundreds of acres at a time, this was a small price to pay for access to these lands and the low level of development in the region. Last, St. Joe's massive landholdings provide a focal point for general concerns about the direction the panhandle is taking. The sheer size of the company's landholdings makes St. Joe a touchstone for public debate. It is likely that if St. Joe's holdings were split among many more landowners, the public response to any development proposals would be significantly less intense. In a strange twist, St. Joe's emergence as a development entity has energized local residents, residents who traditionally viewed planning as a problem and not a solution, to become engaged in planning processes.

CHALLENGE #3: HIGH LEVELS OF POLITICAL INFLUENCE

The final major challenge lies in St. Joe's access to and influence with state and local political and business leaders. St. Joe's status as the largest private landowner in the state and the company's panhandle development plans, which many politicians view strictly as "economic development," have provided numerous connections with county commissioners, state legislators, and the governor's office. In addition, St. Joe is a member of a very influential development lobbying group, the Association of Florida Community Developers (AFCD). The AFCD routinely lobbies for weakening the DRI process, a lesser state role in comprehensive planning, and greater state funding for infrastructure to support development. Members of the AFCD include most of the major homebuilders in the state, as well as law firms and consulting firms that provide services to these large builders.

As a result of this access and influence, St. Joe and the AFCD have had a strong hand in shaping land use and planning legislation in the state. Evidence for this influence can be seen in two policy areas. First, St. Joe and the AFCD lobbied to have the DRI thresholds raised in counties designated as "rural areas of critical economic concern," including Franklin and Gulf counties, where St. Joe has pursued several development projects. In the case of Franklin County, the new DRI threshold was set at 600 residential units. St. Joe's SummerCamp development in Franklin County subsequently came in at 599 residential units and was thus exempted from the DRI process.

Second, in 2006 the Florida legislature passed legislation (HB 1359) pertaining to development within coastal areas of the state. Previously, the state had language that explicitly directed local governments to steer population and development away from "coastal high hazard areas," areas of particularly high risk from hurricane storm damage (Deyle, Chapin, and Baker 2007). Backed heavily by St. Joe, HB 1359 allows more development in these coastal hazard zones if the developer can mitigate the hurricane evacuation impacts of any new development. It also reduces the state's role in limiting development within these areas. Representatives from environmental and planning groups labeled this legislation the "St. Joe Coastal Development Act."

Planning Implications Relating to Large Landowners

Taken as a whole, the St. Joe Company provides a fascinating case from which to examine the planning opportunities and challenges related to large landowners. With landholdings representing roughly 2 percent of Florida's area and ownership of more than half the privately owned land in certain counties in the panhandle, St. Joe is a large landowner on a remarkable scale. The company's development plans only serve to intensify the impacts of these large landholdings. As detailed earlier, St. Joe's development plans are being carried out within the context of Florida's comprehensive planning system, the nation's most detailed state-mandated approach for managing growth. The story of this massive landowner with an active development agenda and local governments and a state land planning agency operating under a state mandate for comprehensive planning makes for an excellent case study of the intersection of large landowners and plan-making processes.

In this chapter I have discussed how a large landowner can positively and negatively influence local and state planning processes. Compared with smaller developers, large landowners like St. Joe bring a very different set of planning opportunities and challenges to the table. In some ways, large landowners represent the most desirable of developers; they have land to spare for infrastructure, public facilities, and environmental protection, and they offer an opportunity to plan at a scale that makes more sense when considering the broader goals of land use planning, infrastructure provision, environmental sustainability, and transportation system planning. The other largely unexpected planning opportunity that emerged from the St. Joe case lay in the ability of the DCA to pursue new regional planning strategies. The DCA believes very strongly in these policy innovations, and the willingness of St. Joe to work through these new planning processes has taught the DCA great lessons about these processes.

Although a landowner like St. Joe offers planning opportunities, these opportunities are counterbalanced by key planning challenges. Foremost among these was the co-optation of the process by a developer interested in plan making as a means to enable its development projects. In addition, the scope of St. Joe's development plans yielded much greater than usual levels of public participation and negativity toward almost any of their development proposals. Similar projects floated by smaller developers typically did not generate the level and intensity of public comment. The other challenge related to St. Joe's status as a major landowner lay in the company's access to and influence with political leaders. St. Joe has often used its connections with state and local leaders to further its development agenda. Although this challenge is not unique to large landowners, St. Joe's large landholdings magnify its political influence.

The St. Joe case reveals a fascinating, if contradictory, position for large landowners when it comes to planning processes and plan-making activities. St. Joe has proved to be an active plan maker, particularly in those cases where its plans can promote the company's development interests. The company has also willingly engaged in innovative planning initiatives, with mixed success. However, at the same time that the company pursued detailed, rigorous, and innovative plan-making initiatives, St. Joe worked behind the scenes to undercut these planning processes. While advocating for better plans in many panhandle communities, St. Joe was actively lobbying to reduce planning requirements for the same areas.

From this evidence, then, a cynical viewpoint emerges, one shared by many residents and panhandle interest groups. St. Joe appears to be interested only in those planning processes and planning documents that can enhance the company's bottom line. This large corporate entity was supportive of public sector–based planning initiatives only when these efforts could positively influence the firm's profit potential. The St. Joe case recalls Fogelsong's investigation (2001) of the Walt Disney Company and its dealings with local governments in central Florida. Where desirable, Disney operated as a public entity with land use and taxing powers the envy of neighboring governments. At other times, Disney retreated into the shadows and acted as a profit-driven, entirely self-interested actor in open conflict with the public sector. Disney's choice in this regard was based not on a vision of a more desirable future for the region, or on an effort to work with others to create a "good society," but instead solely on its determination of what made the most sense for the company's annual financial statements.

A central lesson derived from the St. Joe case study is that a government with large landowners within its jurisdiction should view these landowners as potential assets to plan-making processes. These large landowners offer advantages in achieving goals common to local governments: an ability to plan at a larger scale, to further environmental protection efforts, and to establish a land use pattern that makes sense for the long term. However, the St. Joe case also indicates that public officials and planners need to be aware that private landowners have fundamentally different motivations and interests when it comes to the development and implementation of plans. This case study reveals that the interests of the public sector and those of a large landowner like St. Joe may overlap, but that these interests are not and will likely never be one and the same.

6

PUBLIC SECTOR LAND DEVELOPERS IN NEW DELHI AND BANGALORE, INDIA

A Comparison of Processes and Outcomes

David L. Gladstone and Kameswara Sreenivas Kolapalli

The role of the state in shaping the development of metropolitan areas has been of considerable concern to researchers. This is an especially important issue in the context of third world metropolitan areas, where powerful regional and global economic forces are acting to rapidly change the urban landscape. Public sector planning policies and visions clearly are important for how economics shape such areas. But the public sector can be important beyond setting the rules for development in low-income countries. In many cases, public sector agents control large swaths of land, which allows them to play additional roles, namely, those of developers and arbiters of development.

This chapter examines two cases of large-scale state ownership and development of land. The focus is on Delhi and Bangalore,[1] two Indian cities in which the state plays a major role in land acquisition and development. We have chosen Delhi and Bangalore because although the two cities are characterized by extensive state involvement in land ownership and property development, they differ in important respects. In Delhi, the entire land development process is managed by

1. In late 2006 the Government of Karnataka changed the official name of Bangalore to Bengaluru, the city's precolonial name (*Times of India* 2005b). Because many city and regional agencies still use the word "Bangalore" in their names, because the Government of Karnataka still uses the old name in some of its publications, and because the English spelling of the city ("Bengaluru" versus "Bengalooru") is still in question, we have used the old name here.

the Delhi Development Authority (DDA), a federal planning and land development agency that acquires land through its power of eminent domain and then subdivides and develops the land before disposing of it in the form of apartments (or "flats") or as plots to residential, commercial, and industrial users. In Bangalore, the Government of Karnataka acquires land on a much more limited scale through the Karnataka Industrial Areas Development Board (KIADB), prepares the land for intensive industrial use, and then turns the development sites over to private sector firms, most notably software and computer-related companies.

The structure, goals, and policy tools of the DDA and the KIADB differ as well. Whereas the DDA is a federal agency with broad powers that has intervened heavily in Delhi land markets since the 1950s, the KIADB is a state agency that was relatively unsuccessful in promoting industrial land development until the 1990s. And whereas the DDA still operates as a federal planning bureaucracy, the KIADB operates more like a marketing and development firm than a state agency. The DDA's primary policy goal is managing the growth of Delhi, a goal that DDA planners attempt to realize through their statutory control of urban planning and land development in the city. In Bangalore, the KIADB implements land development policies designed to attract investment from private sector firms, particularly software and electronics firms. Despite very different goals, bureaucratic structures, and policy concerns, the activities of both the DDA and the KIADB have had a marked effect on urban development patterns in Delhi and Bangalore, respectively, not only within the geographic boundaries of each city but on a much larger regional scale.

Finally, it is important to note that the scale of public sector land ownership differs in each city. Although both Delhi and Bangalore are characterized by extensive state ownership and control of land, the state owns or controls much more land in Delhi, where DDA holdings account for close to 15 percent of the city's total land area. In contrast, public sector agencies control much less land in Bangalore and have restricted their activities largely to industrial development on the fringes of the metropolitan area. Nevertheless, we have found that public sector landowners in Bangalore have had a significant impact on the urban structure of the metropolitan area, largely through the ripple effects of large-scale and sustained investments in information technology (IT) industries.

Delhi and Bangalore in Comparative Perspective

Delhi

The National Capital Territory of Delhi (NCTD) consists of Delhi, New Delhi, and Delhi Cantonment, which together cover a land area of about 1,483 square kilometers (NDMC 2005). In addition to its status as a national capital territory, Delhi is also both a state and a city. In 2001 the total population of the NCTD was 13.85 million people, made up of 2.73 million households residing in 2.32 million housing units (NCTD 2005a). The Municipal Corporation of Delhi (the governing municipal structure of Delhi city) is India's second-largest city after Mumbai, with a population of about 9.8 million residents (Office of the Registrar General, India 2002a). Although DDA planners believe that 15.3 million people can be accommodated in the existing urbanized area of 447 square kilometers, they expect the city's population to reach about 22 million by 2021 (DDA 2005).

Delhi's population has increased rapidly over the past 50 years because of large-scale in-migration during the preindependence period, mass migration from the state of Punjab during the 1980s, and migration for employment from the adjoining states of Uttar Pradesh and Haryana and from the northern state of Bihar (DDA 2005; NCRPB 2005; TCPO 1995). Delhi's urbanization rate is 93 percent, making it the most urbanized state in the country (Office of the Registrar General, India 2002a). Urban growth is occurring not only within the geographic boundaries of the NCTD, but also at the city's urban fringe, in the neighboring states of Haryana and Uttar Pradesh. The Delhi Urban Agglomeration (DUA), made up of the NCTD and surrounding municipalities, is among the fastest-growing urban agglomerations in the country (Mookherjee and Hoerauf 2004). The population of the NCTD grew by more than 40 percent during the 1990s, and the satellite towns grew even faster (Mookherjee and Hoerauf 2004; Sivam 2003).

The Government of India created the DDA in 1957 in order to "plan and effect the development of Delhi so as to provide shelter,

amenities and facilities to its existing population and also to make provisions for future growth" (MoUD). Under the Delhi Development
Act of 1957, the DDA is charged with "promot[ing] and secur[ing] the
development of Delhi" and is responsible for land management and
development in the city (DDA a). Since its inception in 1957, the
DDA has acquired over 60,000 acres of land, 96 percent of which it
has developed for various land uses, and the agency has plans to develop more than half the territory of the NCTD (MoUD). The DDA
acquires land at below-market rates, maintains a land bank for future
development, and auctions off land for both residential and nonresidential uses.[2] DDA planners use profits from land sales to subsidize
low-income housing programs (Srirangan 2000).

Scholarly opinion is mixed regarding the effectiveness of agencies
like the DDA. Although some scholars may view public land development and cross-subsidization for economically weaker populations as
effective tools for planned development and for providing land access
to the poor (Srirangan 2000), a general perception among development economists operating out of a neoclassical economic paradigm is
that most state interventions in land markets are counterproductive
and often result in artificially inflated land values, housing shortages,
rent-seeking behavior, and the unplanned growth of squatter settlements. In the case of the DDA, at least some observers have noted the
failure of the agency to provide land to poorer segments of the population. Mitra (2002), for example, found that from 1960 to 1971, higher-
income groups received the lion's share of residential land disbursed
by the DDA. Another more general concern about the effectiveness of
the DDA lies in the role the agency plays in Delhi's overall urban governance (Malpani 2003). Although the DDA is in charge of the city's
land development and management, state and municipal agencies (as
opposed to a national agency like the DDA) such as the Delhi Jal
Board (Delhi Water Board), the Delhi Vidyut Board (Delhi Power
Board), and the Municipal Corporation of Delhi are responsible for

---

2. The DDA develops land for industrial, commercial, and residential uses. For residential developments targeted at higher- and middle-income groups, the DDA allocates flats
through random selection, and for lower-income groups by date of registration (DDA b).
The DDA allocates land for commercial, industrial, and institutional purposes either
through auction or under "Nazul rules," rules that govern the development of land vested
with the state for public purposes (DDA 1981; Rajya Sabha 2005).

providing water, sewerage, electricity, transportation, and other components of the city's infrastructure (Malpani 2003). A multiplicity of agencies operating on different government levels, critics charge, often leads to inefficient outcomes as real estate development activities remain haphazard and uncoordinated.

Another concern is that the huge demand for land, combined with long waiting periods for DDA housing and both residential and commercial building plots, is leading (indeed, has already led) to a proliferation of unauthorized housing colonies and nonconforming commercial uses throughout the city. According to the Tejendra Khanna Committee, a commission set up by the Government of India to evaluate the scope and extent of unauthorized structures in the NCTD, about 25–30 percent of housing in the NCTD is unauthorized, and 80 percent of hospitals, government offices, and educational institutions, as well as a large number of hotels, operate in residential areas (Gladstone 2005; Tejendra Khanna Committee 2006). Furthermore, the committee found that the DDA has been able to construct and provide only 16 percent of the commercial space it has planned for the city (Tejendra Khanna Committee 2006).

Another indirect outcome of DDA activities is rapid and uncontrolled growth of residential and commercial areas along Delhi's periphery, just outside the authority's jurisdictional boundaries. Taking advantage of land shortages in Delhi as well as infrastructure investments within the NCTD that allow relatively fast access to the Delhi central business district (CBD), real estate developers have converted large tracts of agricultural land and scrubland into seas of high-rise residential complexes. Not surprisingly, the outlying towns in the DUA experienced a 212 percent increase in population compared with the 35 percent increase in the core city from 1991 to 2001 (Mookherjee and Hoerauf 2004).[3]

Given supply constraints and rising demand for land in the NCTD, and perhaps also in keeping with the liberalization of the Indian economy begun in the early 1990s under the Narasimha Rao government,

3. India's pattern of urbanization differs from that of many other third world countries because there is no single primate city (Sita and Chatterjee 1990). The central cities of all four metropolitan areas, Delhi, Kolkata (formerly Calcutta), Mumbai (formerly Bombay), and Chennai (formerly Madras), dominate the country's urban structure (Sita and Chatterjee 1990). With the emergence of new commercial and residential centers near Delhi in the 1990s, however, the DUA now proves an exception to the general trend.

the DDA's future plans call for greater involvement of the private sector in residential real estate development and infrastructure provision. DDA plans also include the development of a new "subcity" of Dwarka (13,963 acres) within the NCTD and two satellite townships of Narela (18,208 acres) and Dhirpur (480 acres) (MoUD). DDA planners claim to be focusing heavily on the provision of land and services to lower-income groups, but scholars have at times differed with officials. Kundu (2003), for instance, points out that the DDA's proposed *Master Plan of Delhi—2021* contains more provisions for higher- and middle-income groups to purchase land and to convert their current leasehold interests into freehold interests than provisions to distribute land to people in lower-income groups.

Bangalore

With a population of 4.3 million people and a land area of 226 square kilometers, Bangalore is India's fourth-largest city; only Mumbai, Delhi, and Kolkata (formerly Calcutta) are home to more people (BBMP; Office of the Registrar General, India 2002b). Until the 1960s, however, Bangalore was a relatively small city where family-based land ownership patterns predominated (S. Kumar 2001). Until the 1950s, the city's economy was based on local industries such as silk weaving (Benjamin 2000). Through large and sustained public investment in industrial and defense-related businesses in the 1960s and 1970s, however, the city and surrounding villages grew into a metropolitan area of 6.8 million inhabitants, with numerous software and other IT firms producing for a global market—the city is now known worldwide as the "Silicon Valley of India" (Benjamin 2000; BBMP; Lateef 1997; Nair 2005). Evidence of the city's success in attracting global IT firms is everywhere, ranging from the scores of Western fast-food outlets in the city's commercial areas to the massive new office and research parks housing the new high-technology firms to the exclusive residential areas catering overwhelmingly to foreign workers and nonresident Indians (Benjamin 2000). Higher-paid formal sector employees, many of whom work in the IT sector, have access to land in residential areas developed by the Bangalore Development Authority (BDA) or can afford to purchase luxury apartments developed by private sector builders. There are fewer housing options for the poor and lower middle classes, especially as regards the purchase of residential plots (S. Kumar 2001).

The BDA was established in 1976 by an act of the Karnataka legislature to "plan, regulate, control, monitor and facilitate urban development in Bangalore Metropolitan Area and to ensure sustainable and orderly growth" (BDA). Unlike the DDA, the BDA does not have a near monopoly on large-scale land development; the private sector plays a much greater role in both residential and commercial real estate development activities. And unlike the DDA, the BDA no longer builds apartments ("BDA flats"), restricting its role to land acquisition and site preparation for residential and commercial end users.[4]

The Karnataka State Electronics Development Corporation Limited (KEONICS), now part of Karnataka's Department of Information Technology, was constituted in 1976 by the Government of Karnataka to promote the electronics industry in the state. KEONICS initially acquired about 332 acres of land from the KIADB for the development of KEONICS Electronic City on the southern outskirts of Bangalore (about 18 kilometers from the city center), an area that now forms the hub of the city's IT industry.[5] Major software firms, including the Indian-owned firms Infosys and Wipro and foreign-based firms such as Hewlett-Packard and 3M, have located in Electronic City. The KIADB has transferred an additional 1,400 acres to IT firms in successive phases of Electronic City and in the Export Promotion Industrial Park at Whitefield on the northeastern outskirts of the city (Bangalore Properties 2005). State efforts to allocate an additional 800 acres to an Indian IT firm were blocked by new greenbelt provisions imposed by Bangalore planning authorities as part of the city's comprehensive development plan (CDP), one effect of the city's rapid growth in the 1980s and 1990s (Bangalore Properties 2005).

To attract large-scale investments and reduce bureaucratic hurdles, KEONICS instituted a straightforward procedure for allocating land to industries in Electronic City. Any firm that came forward with a "detailed project report" for its operations and the required approvals

---

4. The BDA ceased its housing operations in the 1980s.

5. KEONICS Electronic City is now known as Electronic City Phase I. The KIADB will develop future phases of Electronic City without the assistance of KEONICS, which now functions as a technology consulting firm.

from statutory bodies would be allocated land at heavily subsidized rates.[6] At first demand for land was lacking; during the early stages of the project, officials would routinely award more land than the firms actually requested because there were few takers at that time. With the influx of software firms into the city during the 1990s, however, the situation changed dramatically, both because the demand for suitable industrial land increased and because the supply did not keep pace with demand.

The IT industry is now driving the office space market not only in Bangalore's CBD, but in non-CBD areas as well, and is exerting a major influence on the city's social structure (*Deccan Herald* 2005). One result of Bangalore's great success in attracting global IT firms is the creation of a dual city of great wealth and great poverty, what Atlas (2005) calls, on one hand, "a burgeoning city of 6 million . . . with typical Third World afflictions" and, on the other hand, a world city characterized by "major outsourcing campuses with modern architecture and landscaping, air-conditioned offices, and cappuccino-serving food courts." Although the number of poor people in Bangalore is greater now than it was 40 years ago, one *BusinessWeek* reporter recently observed that "the most stunning new development in Bangalore is the Adarsh Palm Meadows, an 85-acre California-style gated community complex of commercial, residential, and IT park space" (*BusinessWeek* 2005).

Bangalore's municipal authorities have at times been overwhelmed by the rapid change the city has undergone since the 1960s as it has metamorphosed from a small Indian city to a high-tech boomtown (Lateef 1997). One result of the city's rapid growth has been higher real estate prices; another has been a shortage of developable land close to the city center, which has fueled sprawl on the city's outskirts as IT firms have converted rural acreage into office parks (*Space Daily* 2004). Many of the city's software firms have sprawling campuses and offices in Electronic City as well as in other parts of the Bangalore Urban Agglomeration (BUA), placing additional pressure on city ser-

---

6. Firms interested in acquiring land for development purposes are required to submit, among other things, a deposit of INR 500 per acre up to a maximum of INR 10,000, all the necessary approvals from regulatory agencies, and 20 percent of the land costs along with their applications for an allocation of land (KIADB n.d.). Thus, the amount firms pay for acquiring the land is much less than the market rate.

vices. In an effort to reduce development pressures in Bangalore, government agencies are developing new technology parks and subsidizing IT firms' land acquisition in other parts of the state. Infosys, a large Bangalore-based software firm, has developed a 300-acre campus in Mysore, a smaller city in Karnataka, and has acquired an additional 312 acres in Mangalore (another smaller city in Karnataka) for future development (Bangalore Properties 2005). Wipro, another large software firm based in Bangalore, has also sought to acquire land in both cities (Bangalore Properties 2005).

Points of Comparison

Our initial review of the literature led us to assume that the impact of large public sector landowners in Delhi and Bangalore on urban development patterns would differ because the goals, policy tools, scale of development, and power of the land development agencies differ. In Delhi, the DDA is responsible for the planning and development of the entire NCTD. In Bangalore, the KIADB acquires land and prepares it for final industrial users, but private sector firms play a major role in developing the sites. And unlike the DDA, the KIADB is not charged with promoting socioeconomic equity in the city or region, and it promotes industrial activities with almost negligible input from local administrative agencies like the BDA or Bruhat Bangalore Mahanagara Palike (BBMP).[7] Furthermore, since the DDA is responsible for both the planning and development of the NCTD, we thought it reasonable to assume that the DDA would not promote industrial or commercial uses without first providing the necessary infrastructure and housing, which would lead to more balanced development than in Bangalore. In contrast, we assumed that as Bangalore became a global center of IT, and as private sector firms made huge investments in the city's industrial zones, the cash-starved local housing and social service agencies like the BDA or BBMP would prove ill equipped to meet the demand for housing, infrastructure, and other urban development facilities that the new industrial uses generate. Instead, private real estate developers would cater to the housing needs of higher- and middle-income groups, and the poor and

7. Bruhat Bangalore Mahanagara Palike was once known as the Bangalore City Corporation, or BCC.

even elements of the middle class would make do with substandard housing and infrastructure provided through informal housing markets.

In what follows, we revisit our initial assumptions through a detailed analysis of land development processes in Delhi and Bangalore. We pay particular attention to the outcomes of each process with respect to land markets (price and availability of land), equity (access to land by lower-income groups), infrastructure provision (adequate or inadequate level of services), land-use patterns (types of industrial and residential development), and overall urban development (pace of growth and the role of the central city within the broader regional framework). In the concluding section of this chapter, we consider the degree to which land development patterns and social outcomes in Delhi, where a government agency plays a major role in land acquisition and ownership, differ from those of Bangalore, where a government agency plays a major role in land acquisition and ownership but private firms are the major actors in developing land.

Findings

Land Markets

Delhi

Land prices increased dramatically in the NCTD from 1980 to 1990: real prices increased about 300 to 500 percent in most parts of the city over the course of the decade (see table 6.1). The rapid escalation of land and housing prices is attributable to several factors, including the migration of people into the NCTD, especially from the Punjab and the northern states of Uttar Pradesh and Bihar; speculation; land scarcity because the DDA was not able to meet increased demand from residential and commercial users; and the gradual "opening up" of India during the 1980s to international trade and capital flows. A devalued rupee, in particular, meant higher import costs, which increased inflation throughout the country, including in land markets.

The DDA's average land development costs in 1995 were about INR 335 per square meter, a significant increase over previous decades due in part to increases in the DDA's administrative, land development, and construction costs (TCPO 1995).[8] Despite rapidly escalat-

8. In 1995 the Indian rupee was trading at about 30 rupees to the U.S. dollar, and as of March 2009, the rate was about 50 rupees to the dollar.

Table 6.1   Delhi land values, 1980–1990 (rupees)

Area	Year 1980	Year 1985	Year 1990	Percentage change, 1980–1990
South Delhi	5,776	9,017	27,571	377.3
West Delhi	2,550	5,466	13,973	448.0
East Delhi	1,801	5,634	11,088	515.8
North Delhi	780	1,604	5,348	585.6

Note: All values are in rupees per square meter rounded to the nearest rupee, in constant 1993–1994 rupees.

Source: TCPO (1995).

ing land prices in the NCTD, however, the real cost of DDA apartments for lower-income groups fell about 7 percent during the 1980s, even as costs rose by about 20 percent for the middle-income group (see table 6.2). The drop in the cost of DDA apartments for lower-income groups provides evidence that the DDA was in fact doing what it claimed, namely, providing subsidized housing for lower-income families in the NCTD.

During the 1995–2000 period, nominal land prices fell in Delhi, although not nearly as much as they had risen during the 1980s (see table 6.3). Factors fueling the decline in land prices include the greater availability of land in neighboring states outside the authority of the DDA in the Delhi Metropolitan Area (DMA) fringe towns of Gurgaon, Ghaziabad, Noida, and Faridabad and national (nonlocal) factors such as the Bombay Stock Exchange crash of the late 1990s and the corresponding decline in land prices in the country's major metropolitan regions.[9] In the 2000s, however, land values increased throughout the NCTD once again, before markets crashed in the aftermath of the 2008 global financial crisis. Developable land, even in DMA fringe areas, has become relatively scarce.

As some scholars note, rising Delhi land prices have been due to the DDA's monopolistic land policies and its inability to meet residential and business demand for land. Because the DDA was unable to supply the land required for the commercial and residential development needs of the NCTD, settlements on the city's periphery began to develop with the participation of private sector corporate real estate firms (TCPO 1995). People who could not afford land in Delhi shifted to

9. During the 1994–1998 period, land prices in the fringe town of Gurgaon increased nearly 300 percent (N. Kumar 2003).

Table 6.2   DDA apartment values, 1981–1991 (rupees)

Income group	Year			Percentage change, 1981–1991
	1981	1987	1991	
Lower	966	718	898	−7.1
Middle	1,119	816	1,351	20.7

Note: Apartment value is the purchase price per square meter. All values are rounded to the nearest rupee, in constant 1993–1994 rupees.

Source: TCPO (1995).

Table 6.3   Delhi housing values, 1995–2000 (rupees)

Area	1995	1998	2000	Percentage change, 1995–2000
Central Delhi	78,691	52,739	42,096	−46.5
West Delhi	39,345	22,040	17,540	−55.4
East Delhi	14,754	7,871	7,016	−52.4

Note: All values are in rupees per square meter rounded to the nearest rupee, in constant 1993–1994 rupees.

Source: N. Kumar (2003).

the DMA fringe towns within close proximity to the city center, where land costs were significantly lower (N. Kumar 2003; TCPO 1995).[10]

DDA policies designed to regulate land development in the NCTD also provided an opportunity for land developers and municipal administrators in outlying areas to promote development activity just outside the DDA's jurisdiction. They were able to benefit from the development activities, especially the infrastructure development, undertaken by the DDA in the NCTD but were not subject to the DDA's near monopoly on land acquisition and development activity or its planning controls. Thus, as we have noted, the satellite towns of Faridabad, Noida, Gurgaon, and Ghaziabad, which have good transportation and communication links to the international and domestic airports as well as to the Delhi city center, grew much faster than the NCTD during the 1990s.[11]

10. Even though land scarcity in the NCTD and the accompanying increases in land prices led to an outflow of development activities to fringe areas, the ability to secure land in fringe towns at a lower cost than in the NCTD has led to speculation in the fringe areas.

11. The difference in land prices in Delhi and surrounding areas goes far in accounting for the development trajectories of the satellite townships that ring the central city. In 1998

BANGALORE

The KIADB has acquired and developed about 8,960 acres of land in over 21 industrial areas in the Bangalore district since the late 1960s. It has allocated nearly 75 percent of the land (6,600 acres) to industrial users and close to 10 percent to IT, information technology and enabled services (ITES), and electronics industry firms (KIADB 2006a, 2006b). The prevailing market rate for industrial properties citywide ranged in 2006 from about INR 1.2 million per acre to about INR 8.0 million per acre, and the cost of land in Electronic City and the Export Promotion Industrial Park, Phase I and Phase II, which predominantly houses IT, ITES, and electronics industry firms, ranged from INR 4 million to INR 8 million per acre (KIADB 2006a). According to Electronic City Industrial Association officials, the market rate of land in Electronic City is higher than the rates charged by the KIADB, so the Government of Karnataka is subsidizing the land acquisition costs of IT and other high-technology firms.

The rapid growth of the city's IT and related electronics industries has driven up land costs in Bangalore in both direct and indirect ways. Industrial land in the country's booming IT hub of Bangalore was in high demand through the fall of 2008, which is reflected in the fact that since the beginning of 2000, the KIADB has allocated nearly 40 percent of all the land it has ever allocated or reallocated.[12] The increased demand for industrial land has reverberated throughout the city's land economy and has, at least through 2008, translated into higher residential and commercial property rates in all parts of the metropolitan area. During 2003 alone, developers added about 630,000 square meters of commercial space to the Bangalore Metro-

---

land prices in Delhi ranged from about INR 3,000 to INR 7,500 per square meter; during the same period, land prices in Noida, a satellite township, were about INR 1,200 to INR 6,000 per square meter. Land prices in Ghaziabad, another of Delhi's satellite townships, were even lower, ranging from INR 800 to INR 4,000 per square meter (N. Kumar 2003). The significant price differential explains, at least in part, why population as well as industrial and commercial development has shifted to Delhi's outskirts and away from the core of the DMA. Another reason for the rapid growth of the satellite townships is the infrastructure provided by the DDA and other authorities in Delhi—for example, the Delhi Metro, the outer ring road, and the new highway connecting Gurgaon to the international airport—which has increased the connectivity of the satellite townships to the central city.

12. Before the IT boom, lending agencies would at times foreclose on industrial plots sold by the KIADB (Kodandapani 2005b).

politan Region (BDA 2005).[13] Fueled by the demands of IT managers and workers, the real price of residential building plots increased significantly from 2001 to 2006 in the metropolitan region—from 100 percent to over 200 percent in areas closer to the high-technology parks (for example, in JP Nagar and Koramangala, respectively) (see table 6.4). Even the assessed government rates for land in areas close to the industrial parks increased significantly from 1996 to 2006 (see table 6.5).[14]

Table 6.4   Bangalore land values, selected areas, 2001–2006 (rupees)

Area	Year						Percentage change, 2001–2006
	2001	2002	2003	2004	2005	2006	
Bannerghatta	787	914	1,052	1,249	1,270	1,759	123.4
Hosur Road	787	853	935	1,022	1,081	1,759	123.4
Indira Nagar	1,260	1,218	1,286	1,419	1,513	3,224	155.9
JP Nagar	819	914	994	568	1,243	1,641	100.5
Jaya Nagar	961	1,096	1,228	1,306	1,513	2,345	144.1
Koramangala	787	1,218	1,345	1,419	1,486	2,638	235.0
Whitefield	740	670	789	852	973	1,759	137.6

Note: All values are in rupees per square foot rounded to the nearest rupee, in constant 1993–1994 rupees.
Source: Undisclosed Bangalore real estate development firm.

Table 6.5   Bangalore assessed property values, selected areas, 1996–2006 (rupees)

Area	Distance from IT park (miles)*	Year				Percentage change, 1996–2006
		1996	1998	2001	2006	
JP Nagar	10	398	314	271	997	150.3
Jaya Nagar	7	251	N/A	N/A	1,055	319.6
Koramangala	15	419	439	378	1,143	172.8
Whitefield	3	126	102	88	293	133.1

Note: All values are in rupees per square foot rounded to the nearest rupee, in constant 1993–1994 rupees.
* For JP Nagar and Jaya Nagar, the distance is from Electronic City; for Koramangala and Whitefield, the distance is from Export Promotion Industrial Park. All distances are approximate.
Source: Anonymous (1997); Puliani (2005); Simha (1999, 2001).

13. According to 2003 data, shopping centers totaling about 574,000 square feet are in the planning stages; there is already 920,000 square feet of shopping space (Kamala 2003).

14. Government land rates in India are similar to assessed values in the United States and are used primarily for tax-related purposes. Kodandapani (2005a) provides a salient example of the great demand for affordable residential land in Bangalore. After the BDA announced that it was accepting applications for 20,000 sites in one of its affordable housing schemes, it received close to 250,000 applications.

Land prices increased not only in areas close to the industrial parks, but in almost all parts of the Bangalore Metropolitan Area (BMA) over the decade ending in 2008. With more industrial units planned as part of the state government's industrial promotion policy, and as the market for real estate continued to boom, real estate developers and property consultants in the city predicted an abnormal increase in the market rates for all categories of property. Vagale (2002) notes that the growth of the city and accompanying real estate speculation led in the early 2000s to an inversion of the ratio of land value to construction costs, from about 1:4.5 to about 4.5:1.

Social Structure and Land Use Patterns

DELHI

Although the DDA provides housing for all income groups, its efforts have not been sufficient to meet the needs of all Delhiites. Out of the two million households in the NCTD area, nearly half live in non-DDA structures and many reside in unauthorized structures, in either jhuggi-jhopri clusters or unauthorized colonies (DUEIIP 2001).[15] The problems stem from an inadequate supply of DDA housing and a lack of affordable private sector housing, which is in turn a result of the rapid escalation of land prices in Delhi since the early 1980s, at least through the end of 2008 (NCTD 2005a, 2005c; TCPO 1995). Even the Delhi government finds it difficult to provide housing for its employees, since adequate numbers of houses at affordable rates are simply not available. In 2005, for example, only 6,067 houses were available for 125,000 government employees.[16]

---

15. In 1994 about 9.5 square kilometers of land, worth over $14 billion, was occupied by squatters and slums (Basu and Bhandari n.d.). About 1.8 million Delhiites live in slums, but Municipal Corporation of Delhi field surveys indicate a much larger slum population of more than 1,100 jhuggi-jhopri clusters housing close to three million people (NCTD 2005b, 2005c).

16. The housing shortage has become so acute in Delhi that the state government of Delhi now plans to construct its own housing for employees (NCTD 2005a). Government officials have formed the Delhi Social Housing and Infrastructure Development Corporation to provide housing for lower-income groups and slum residents (NCTD 2005a). Although it is not clear how the government plans to acquire land and gain the necessary approvals from the DDA to undertake these developments, the very existence of the plans is clear evidence of the need for more housing in the city.

Because of land price inflation and a shortage of housing in the city, the Delhi Urban Art Commission (DUAC) has called for reductions in plot sizes in the Lutyens Bungalow Zone close to the city center, an area that is home to many high-ranking government of-

According to a Town and Country Planning Organisation (TCPO) report on land policies in Delhi (1995), only 44,446 plots (about 26 percent of the total) were allocated to lower-income groups by the DDA through 1994, and the DDA allocated only 3.9 percent of the plots in higher-income areas to lower-income beneficiaries (see table 6.6). Given that there are more than one million households below the poverty line in the NCTD, the supply of housing is clearly not sufficient to meet the needs of the population. Moreover, the plots allocated to lower-income groups by the DDA range in cost from about INR 260 per square meter to INR 360 per square meter, much more than in other cities and clearly not affordable to those sections of the population for which they are intended (TCPO 1995). A similar trend is the disposal of apartments constructed by the DDA from 1967 to 1995. According to DDA data, the agency allotted about 61 percent of the 244,295 apartments to lower-income groups (TCPO 1995). On average, the lower-income apartments cost (in 1992 prices) about INR 6,000 per square meter, an amount comparable to the cost of middle-income apartments (about INR 6,160 per square meter).

In part because of a lack of adequate administrative mechanisms and in part because of what some have termed a lack of political interest in providing housing to lower-income groups, one could conceivably argue that DDA land allocation policies have led to the growth of

Table 6.6   DDA distribution of plots by income group, through 1994

Category	Plots		Area	
	Number	Percentage	Acres	Percentage
Lower-income groups	44,446	55	520	27
Middle-income groups	16,123	20	450	23
Alt. allotment	7,999	10	322	16
Auction	12,951	16	670	34
Total	81,519	100	1,962	100

Note: The percentages may not sum to 100, because of rounding error.
Source: TCPO (1995).

ficials (Singh 2007). The plan put forth by the DUAC recommends a uniform land area of one acre for all the plots in the zone. Many plots currently exceed one acre and can be as large as eight acres. The freed-up land will be used for new residential development (Singh 2007). Singh (2007) notes that the plan "has come up against stiff opposition from the urban development ministry, which has asked DUAC to give 'adequate justification' for such sweeping changes."

informal slum settlements and other informal land development and to a socially segregated city (Kundu and Kundu 2006). Another related result is the growth of three parallel land markets in Delhi: subsidized DDA housing and commercial facilities, an organized and regulated private sector land market, and a large unorganized sector of squatter settlements and slums in which people lack clear title to the plots on which they live.

BANGALORE

Although by some accounts Bangalore is among India's best cities for living, working, and investing (Nagarajan 2006), like many other large cities in the South it has numerous slums and a large slum population. The city's slum population increased from about 200,000 in the 1980s to nearly one million in 2006 (BDA 1985; KSCB 2006a). Of the estimated 180,000 households in city slums, only 4,400 are covered under the proposed Valmiki Ambedkar Awas Yojana (VAMBAY) Housing Program, a slum resettlement program supported by the Government of India and the state government (KSCB 2006b). Factors behind the rapid growth of the city's slum population include migration to the city from rural areas and a shortage of affordable formal sector housing.

Like the DDA in Delhi, the BDA lacks the resources to meet the growing market requirements for housing in the city and, as we have pointed out, has stopped building housing altogether (Hussain 2004). And as in Delhi, a lack of affordable housing in the city has resulted in the growth of unauthorized housing developments in many areas,[17] including in middle- and higher-income areas just outside the city's boundaries, where developers find it easier to bypass city development regulations (Kodandapani 2005c). In addition, much of the new construction is in the city's greenbelt and is affordable only to higher-income groups (Kodandapani 2005c). California-style sprawl is therefore contributing to the environmental deterioration of the BMA as it further marginalizes the poor.[18]

17. Unauthorized by the BDA, that is.

18. The Committee on State Urbanization Policy (2002), appointed by the Government of Karnataka to propose guidelines for state urbanization policy, identified the housing shortage for lower- and middle-income groups and proposed that the BDA give land to housing cooperative societies at reduced prices and frame new regulations governing land acquisition for public housing schemes. The committee also proposed that the KIADB consider developing housing schemes for workers in the city's IT parks and other industrial areas.

Infrastructure Provision

DELHI

As both Malpani (2003) and DUEIIP (2001) note, many of Delhi's major planning problems are related to the multitude of organizations that oversee various aspects of infrastructure provision and land development. For example, the Delhi Jal (Water) Board, the Delhi Vidyut (Power) Board, and the Municipal Corporation of Delhi—not the DDA—are in charge of providing essential city services to both developed housing colonies and unauthorized settlements.[19] The multiplicity of organizations and service providers often results in a lack of coordination in the provision of services with the DDA and other land developers in the city, and in many cases infrastructure provision is not up to code. The Indian and the NCTD governments estimate that less than 40 percent of the city's sewage is treated, and solid waste management is grossly inadequate (DUEIIP 2001). Furthermore, about 30 percent of the residential colonies in Delhi have noise levels exceeding international standards, 40 percent of city residents lack an adequate water supply, and 45 percent live without a proper sewage system (DUEIIP 2001). The situation is worse in resettlement colonies and slum areas where, according to Banerji (2005, 5), "90% of the sample households in the slums and 50% of the sample households in resettlement colonies do not have access to independent toilets." Banerji (2005) reports that most of the resettlement colonies are located near highways, away from the places of work, and that most lack access to transportation facilities.

On the positive side, however, are major infrastructure projects that hold out the promise of relieving traffic congestion and may partially alleviate the housing shortage in the capital region and surrounding areas. One is the Delhi Mass Rapid Transit System (MRTS), or Delhi Metro, a massive undertaking planned and constructed by the state- and city-owned Delhi Metro Rail Corporation (DMRC) with the two major aims of providing transportation facilities throughout the DMA and improving environmental conditions in the city (DMRC a). The Delhi Metro is also a vital force in shaping urban development patterns in the city and the larger metropolitan region; real estate devel-

---

19. It is a long-standing demand of the Delhi state government that all the agencies responsible for urban governance in the city be under its purview (*Times of India* 2007a).

opment patterns are changing in many of the urban areas linked with the CBD and other commercial and business districts through the Delhi Metro. The Delhi Metro itself is investing heavily in the property sector at its stations and along rail corridors, seeking to capture the externalities its development generates in the form of land price increases (DMRC b; Siemiatycki 2006).

A second major project is the Delhi-Gurgaon Highway, an elevated toll road that will connect Delhi to the airport and Gurgaon, a rapidly growing edge city in the neighboring state of Haryana. According to the *Times of India* (2005a), "once open, the expressway will offer eight elevated lanes that will only be open to fast-moving traffic with an average of at least 80 km/hr and heavy vehicles travelling over long distances," and slower-moving traffic will use ten additional lanes underneath the elevated roadway. Other highway projects include a four-lane expressway connecting Delhi with Noida and Greater Noida, two rapidly growing towns in the neighboring state of Uttar Pradesh.

For its part, the DDA is now developing land for residential and commercial activities in Dwarka, a semi-agricultural area between Delhi's downtown and the airport, but within the NCTD. With access to the Delhi Metro and therefore within commuting distance of central Delhi, Dwarka is already exhibiting the beginnings of large-scale residential development, mainly adjacent to Delhi Metro stations, and these developments hold out the promise of easing the city's housing shortage.

Bangalore

The *Times of India* (2007b) recently reported on "Bangalore Envy," a term describing the "movement of much of the world's smart money to where many of the world's smart people are." The author of the article claims that the term is the newest in a long line of names for Bangalore, including "Pensioner's Paradise, Lake City, Silicon Capital, Garden City, Corporate City, Young City, Pub City and Healthcare Hub." Yet, however envious people in other cities are of Bangalore and the capital investment that flows there, city residents must cope with widespread deficiencies in water supply and drainage, solid waste management, roads, transportation, and other infrastructure (Vagale 2002).

Like Delhi, Bangalore has inadequate infrastructure facilities because of a rapid increase in population since the 1980s. Many of the unauthorized developments in the fringe areas and in the Bangalore Municipal Corporation area do not have adequate road networks, and only 16 percent of the total road network is paved (Benjamin 2006). The city's transportation network and traffic is chaotic: traveling only a few kilometers may require several hours during peak traffic hours.[20] It can take nearly three hours during peak traffic times to travel from the city center to either Electronic City or the Export Promotion Industrial Park at Whitefield, both of which house many IT firms and are located only 20 kilometers from the city center. Rough estimates show that INR 60 billion (about US$1.5 billion) is required to upgrade the infrastructure to adequate standards (Hussain 2004).

Despite the lack of accessible and fast routes to the city center, infrastructure in the industrial areas, especially the Electronic City and Export Promotion Industrial Park areas, is much better than that of other parts of Bangalore, and this difference parallels the growing divide between better-off and worse-off sections of the city's population. The industrial areas generally have good road and transportation networks, along with sidewalks and other pedestrian amenities. All the industrial areas receive an adequate supply of water, have working sewage systems, and have access to transportation services. The critical issue of accessibility may be partially addressed by two new road projects currently in the planning stages: a partially elevated expressway that will connect Electronic City to the city center and another ring road that will connect the IT parks to each other.

Overall Urban Development

DELHI

Delhi's population more than doubled during the 1981–2001 period, increasing from 6.22 million to 13.85 million (Office of the Registrar General, India 2002b; TCPO 1995). The city's population increase exceeds that of all the other major metropolitan regions in the country, and Delhi continues to attract migrants from the northern and eastern states of Uttar Pradesh, Haryana, Punjab, Rajasthan, and Bihar (NCRPB 1999b). Population increases in the Delhi region are occurring not only in urban areas but in rural and semi-urban areas of the

20. The Electronic City Industrial Association built a fire station on-site out of concern that fire trucks would take too long to reach their destinations.

NCTD as well. Even though Delhi still accounts for a major share of the population increase in the NCTD, the satellite towns of Gurgaon, Faridabad, Noida, and Ghaziabad grew even more rapidly than the NCTD during the 1981–2001 period. In fact, the population growth rates in the satellite towns were almost double that of Delhi during the 1991–2001 period (Office of the Registrar General, India 2002b). Industrial investment during the 25-year period 1971–1996 increased from INR 1.9 billion to about INR 25.2 billion, paving the way for the large numbers of industrial workers who arrived in the Delhi region from neighboring states (NCRPB 1999a, 1999b).

It is clear from the large number of unauthorized settlements dotting the city that the DDA has been unable to provide housing facilities for many immigrants and members of other lower-income groups. The Tejendra Khanna Committee, charged by the Indian government with examining the unauthorized settlements in the NCTD, found the situation alarming. The committee found that it takes on average about 15–20 years to receive an allocated plot from the DDA and that the DDA has built only 16 percent of the commercial space its plans call for (Tejendra Khanna Committee 2006). The committee also notes that 25–30 percent of the housing in the NCTD is unauthorized by the DDA.[21] Meanwhile, the city continues to grow faster than planners projected. DDA planners, in their master plan for 2001 (written in the early 1990s), projected an urbanized area of 48,777 hectares, and the National Capital Region Planning Board's regional plan for 2001 (also written in the 1990s) projected an urbanized area of 62,777 hectares (NCRPB 1999a). By 2001, however, the city's built-up area already exceeded 70,000 hectares, which is larger than the area projected by the planning board only 10 years earlier for the entire metropolitan region (NCRPB 2005).

BANGALORE

Over the past 50 years, Bangalore has grown from a "sleepy town" and retirement center to a major urban agglomeration of nearly five million residents (BDA 1985, 2005). The city's population increased at a rate of 3 percent per year between 1981 and 2001, and some observers estimate that the city's population will exceed 10 million residents by 2015, far surpassing projections made by the BDA in recent years

21. In 1994 there were over 1,300 unauthorized colonies in the NCTD (TCPO 1995).

(BDA 2005; Kodandapani 2005a). In fact, the 1995 revised comprehensive development plan (CDP) projects a population of nearly 7 million in the year 2011 (BDA 1995; BMRDA 2006), and 90 percent of this population target was already achieved by 2001. Bangalore Metropolitan Regional Development Authority planners predict a population in the BMA region of 8 million people, compared with the BDA's projection of 8.5 million, by the year 2011. Given the present level of industrial development and the associated population influx into the area, the population likely will far exceed both projections (Kodandapani 2005a).

As with population growth, so too with urbanization: Bangalore's urban development area exceeded the area projected in both the 2001 and 2011 development plans. In the 2001 plan (written in 1985), planners designated about 220 square kilometers as urban. Planners in subsequent plans (in 1995) increased the figure to 449 square kilometers (BDA 1985, 1995). In 2006 the urban area was roughly 512 square kilometers, which greatly exceeded the projections of earlier city planners (BDA 2005).

Regional planners project an additional 414,000 industrial jobs and an industrial land requirement of 3,351 hectares in the BMA by the year 2011 (BMRDA 2006). Planners estimate that 50 percent of the industrial land will be required for medium-sized and large industrial units (BMRDA 2006). In light of the industrial development of the Bangalore region since the late 1980s, some may argue that the planners have underestimated employment and land requirements since continued global demand for IT services, and Bangalore's comparative advantage in producing them, is only going to increase in coming decades, despite cyclical downturns in the global economy.

Large-scale acquisitions of land for industrial uses will likely lead to further shortages of housing for lower-income groups. During the 1968–2006 period, the KIADB allocated about 2,697 hectares for industrial units, more than half of which it allocated after 1991, as we have noted. A good deal of the land went to IT, ITES, and electronics industry users, which in turn has had a dramatic effect on the city's land use patterns and overall development trajectory through the increase in work participation rates.[22] The 2001 plan and the 2011 re-

22. In fact, the change in the work participation rate in Bangalore during the 1987–2000 period is among the highest of all metropolitan regions in India (Mahadevia 2006).

vised plan both project a housing shortage of more than 10 percent of the existing stock (BDA 1985, 1995). Hussain (2006) estimates that there is a shortage of more than 1.65 million housing units in the Bangalore metropolitan region and that by 2011 the housing shortage will still stand at 1.35 million units (Hussain 2006). As in Delhi, the housing shortage and the increase in population, combined with the slow pace of finalizing site plans by the BDA, have led to many unauthorized settlements and unauthorized construction activity in the city (Hussain 2004; Kodandapani 2005c).

Conclusions

Evaluating the effects of large-scale public sector landowners in Delhi and Bangalore is complicated by the different roles played by the land development agencies in each city. In Delhi, large-scale land development is managed by the DDA for all types of land uses, but in Bangalore, the KIADB plays a major role in land development for industrial uses only. In both cases, public sector agencies act as key players in acquiring large tracts of land, but they employ different methods to acquire and develop the land for final users. Perhaps most importantly, like most cities, both Delhi and Bangalore are subject to strong external (national and international) pressures that severely limit the ability of any public sector land development agency to make lasting improvements in the lives of city residents.

With those caveats out of the way, our analysis indicates that even though land development processes in Delhi and Bangalore differ, both have resulted in higher land prices, rapid changes in land use, and increasing pressure on existing infrastructure. Of great social importance is what appears to be an increasing marginalization of the poor in each city through reductions in the land available to lower-income groups. As Kundu (2003) notes in the case of Delhi, even on the city's periphery, a 21-square-meter plot (the minimum plot size that is both politically and socially acceptable) with access to city services (electricity, water, sewer) costs about INR 120,000 (US$2,400) at 2009 market prices, rendering the provision of land for all slum dwellers beyond the means of the governing authorities, even over a 10-year period. S. Kumar (2001) found a similar marginalization of the poor in Bangalore.

It also seems clear that changes in the land use and urban development patterns of both cities are attributable, at least in part, to the land development policies of the DDA and KIADB. In Delhi DDA policies limit the role of private sector land development in the NCTD, fueling land speculation and sprawl on the city's outskirts, where private sector developers often form virtual land development monopolies (or certainly oligopolies) in towns like Gurgaon. Similarly, in Bangalore, where state authorities have less control over land use decisions, the success of Electronic City and other IT parks fueled large-scale residential developments by private sector real estate developers both within the city limits and in peri-urban areas. Rapid growth on both Delhi's and Bangalore's peripheries is associated with speculation and market volatility, as well as increased traffic congestion, which has led to calls for the development of satellite cities in the DUA and large residential developments closer to sources of employment centers in Bangalore.

Another indirect result of the DDA's and KIADB's activities has been the creation of multiple land markets. In Delhi, nearly a third of NCTD housing is unauthorized, as are nearly 80 percent of hospitals, government offices, educational institutions, and hotels (Tejendra Khanna Committee 2006). Strict planning controls combined with a shortage of residential building plots and apartments have resulted in the growth of three distinct land markets: an organized land market primarily for upper-income groups, a land market of unauthorized structures for both rich and poor, and a speculative land market in urban fringe areas.

In Bangalore, the housing crisis is in many ways a by-product of the city's high-tech economy, which is in turn traceable to the growth of large-scale subsidized industrial parks along the city's perimeter. Since the IT industry has established itself in Bangalore, income inequality in the city has grown dramatically. The income differential between the lowest- and highest-income groups in the city increased from 1:5 to nearly 1:50 during the 1990s (Benjamin 2006). Furthermore, planned areas in the city, where most of the middle- and higher-income residents live, account for only 10 to 25 percent of the city's land area, and much of the land acquired by the state's land development agencies for the large high-technology parks is taken from poor farmers (Benjamin 2006; Benjamin et al. 2006). As in Delhi, therefore, large-scale public sector land ownership has resulted in the growth of three different land markets: an organized private sector market for higher- and middle-income groups in the city itself, an organized private sector market in urban fringe areas (which the BDA claims is unauthorized), and an unauthorized market catering primarily to lower-income residents.

Our investigation also revealed significant differences between the two cities. Although there are shortages of organized (public and private) housing for all income groups in Delhi, and especially for lower-income groups, the situation is not as acute as it is in Bangalore, where the BDA has not built public sector housing since the 1980s and where the private sector has not proved able or willing to build quality housing for lower- and lower-middle-income households. Another difference between the two cities is the level of infrastructure provision. We found that despite serious problems with infrastructure provision in the NCTD, the situation is not nearly as dire in Delhi as it is in Bangalore, where less than 20 percent of the road network is paved and city authorities are only now planning for a rapid mass transit system. (The Delhi Metro began operations in the early 2000s.) A third difference between the two cities is the DDA's ability to better balance the growth of residential, commercial, and industrial uses with adequate infrastructure provision, an outcome we attribute to the DDA's overarching planning and development functions and the fact that the DDA is less focused than the KIADB on industrial development.

CONCLUSION

The six chapters of this volume use the frame of large landowners to study land use and policy from many varied perspectives and in many different contexts. The analytical focus ranges from industry clusters to groups of individual agents to public sector agencies to individual actors, and the approaches range from qualitative case studies to sophisticated empirical and statistical analyses. Each chapter demonstrates the important role that a particular large landowner plays for its local community or region.

Beyond the insights for particular large landowners and particular communities, the chapters also collectively demonstrate that large landowners represent a compelling class of institutions and individuals that merits considerable research attention. As do all landowners, large landowners have the ability to explicitly choose the extent to which they engage along key dimensions that influence land use and policy. However, unlike smaller landowners' choices, the choices of large landowners will almost always be externally important for determining subsequent land uses and ultimately broader community success or failure. This is because their size and scale give large landowners more influence over the course of events and subsequent developments.

The chapters in this volume clearly make this point along the three dimensions examined here. Cosmas Ikejiofor, in chapter 2, and Pengyu Zhu and Raphael W. Bostic, in chapter 1, directly acknowledge the important role that large landowners can play regarding land supply, but land supply considerations are at the forefront in the other chapters as well. In their chapter on Delhi and Bangalore, David L. Gladstone and Kameswara Sreenivas Kolapalli explain that the two main large landowners—the Dehli Development Authority and the Karnataka Industrial Area Development Board—control large swaths of land and make explicit decisions on how to allocate it. Timothy S. Chapin explains that the St. Joe Company adopted a formal strategy to make its land available for development and articulated plans indicating which portions would be reserved for particular land uses. John C. Brown and Jacqueline Geoghegan observe that Clark University made the choice not to limit the supply of land by creating a land buffer between its campus and the surrounding neighborhood in Worcester. And the research question posed by Bostic, LaVonna B. Lewis, and David C. Sloane in chapter 3 is motivated by the ability of hospitals to deliver their services without needing the expansive landholdings that they originally required.

In terms of economics, the two chapters in part 3 show how large landowners can shape the economies of their proximate communities. However, economics is present throughout the volume. Both Ikejiofor, in chapter 2, and Zhu and Bostic, in chapter 1, document how large landowners respond or choose not to respond to economic forces, and provide an indication of how variation in this decision by individual large landowners will shape the evolution of local and regional economies. Gladstone and Kolapalli show that large landowners and economics interact in India in complex ways. In Bangalore, large landowners seek to promote economic development and growth as the primary and unchallenged goal. In Delhi, by contrast, there is more of an acknowledgment that growth comes with costs, and so large landowners seek to mitigate these costs and manage economic development to minimize future costs. Chapin's chapter on the St. Joe Company mirrors Gladstone and Kolapalli's chapter in this regard: St. Joe simultaneously pursues growth to create new prosperity and negotiates with public officials and the community to mitigate and minimize the costs of this growth.

Finally, planning is clearly an important focus of the Chapin and the Gladstone and Kolapalli chapters. But it is also significant for the large landowners that are the focus of the other chapters as well. Brown and Geoghegan highlight the active planning by the University Park Partnership to develop and execute a strategy to broadly improve the Main South community in Worcester. In the chapter on hospitals by Bostic, Lewis, and Sloane, the corridor and cluster agglomeration patterns observed reflect the direct effect of planning on land use and the location of economic activity. For the large fringe landowners in the four U.S. metropolitan areas surveyed in Zhu and Bostic's chapter, restrictions established by planning were a key consideration when deciding whether and how to make their land available for integration into the broader regional developed landscape. In the Ikejiofor chapter, we find that large landowners at the fringe in Enugu, Nigeria, actually faced few planning restrictions regarding the disposition of their land. Rather, these dispositions created the initial framework through which future planning for these lands would take place.

As noted earlier, though, these three dimensions are but examples of the issues arising with large landowners. Across the six chapters of the volume, other overarching points of commonality emerge. For example, there is the issue of whether large landowners become a focal point for energy and activity much as a pole would, or whether they separate and isolate themselves to become something more like an enclave. Clark University and both the KIADB and DDA chose to become poles for their communities. As documented by Perry and Wiewel (2005) and deAragão, Martins, and Neto (2007), there are other large landowners who have opted for the enclave model. Both poles and enclaves are present in the studies of large fringe landowners, hospitals, and the St. Joe Company, which suggests the importance of local and organizational context.

The varying large landowner responses to the choice of whether to act as a pole or enclave raise a number of important questions. First, what are the key factors or contextual features that seem to drive a large landowner's choice to become either a pole for the community or an enclave? What are the benefits of having a large landowner as a community pole? Are there situations in which large landowner isolation as an enclave might be preferred to integration with the neighborhood? These and other questions can add richness to our understanding of land use, community and economic development, and neighborhood dynamics, among other areas.

A second overarching issue is the extent of engagement with the surrounding community. The research by Chapin, Gladstone, and Kolapalli and by Brown and Geoghegan examines large landowners who actively engaged their community. Motivations for this engagement varied—St. Joe sought corporate profits, whereas Clark University and the Indian governmental agencies both had broader social and economic objectives—but the general approach was the same: be present as a visible contributor to the planning and public decision-making processes. By contrast, the large landowners in Enugu, Nigeria, and the hospitals in Los Angeles were decidedly passive in the way that they engaged with the broader community. In these instances, the agents focused largely on individual interests and were not perceived as having leverage regarding public planning and decision making.

The variation in the extent of large landowner engagement observed in this volume points to clear research questions that warrant further study. For example, what determines whether a large landowner, or any entity, decides to engage as an active player or withdraw into a more passive position? Is it possible to identify one approach as dominating the other, such that institutions should always select one course? Or, as in the pole-versus-enclave dichotomy, does context matter? If so, a goal of future research might be to develop a typology that provides guidance for when active or passive engagement is preferable. This would assist both private actors as well as public agencies in working through issues associated with land use and policy decisions.

In this context, one could also gain insights regarding conflict resolution in public arenas. Chapin's study highlights the sometimes contentious relationship between a large landowner and other constituent interests in the community. Brown and Geoghegan, on the other hand, document the highly collaborative effort between Clark University and its neighbors, which ultimately resulted in the creation of a joint organization that managed any internal conflicts directly. Moreover, though it was not the focus of their work, Gladstone and Kolapalli document a process, particularly in Bangalore, in which the public agencies explicitly choose winners and losers, implying an internal conflict resolution process.

Conflict is more likely to arise in public proceedings regarding land use when large landowners are involved, in part because of the usually significant landholdings involved and in part out of local fear of influence peddling by large landowners. Consequently, the study of large landowners in their many different contexts may allow for a deeper understanding of the nature of the conflicts and how certain aspects can ease or inhibit resolution. In sum, the study of large landowners can potentially produce many insights that could ultimately improve conflict resolution processes and help achieve outcomes amenable to all parties involved.

A further area of study is closely related to the issue of conflict resolution and might be a key consideration for improving our understanding of resolution. There are many interests at play in any community—individual, corporate, neighborhood, nonprofit, investor—and balancing these interests is important in an accounting of costs and benefits associated with a particular decision. In any situation, a large landowner can represent a single interest or simultaneously promote multiple interests, a reality reflected in the studies of the large landowners featured in this volume. For example, whereas the Nigerian large landholders in Enugu acted primarily on the basis of their own personal and familial needs, Clark University officials recognized that their self-interest was best served by advancing the interests of the community, individuals, and public sector players.

Understanding the interests considered and represented by large landowners can be an important step in conducting broader benefit-cost analyses of particular land use policies and decisions. Thus, again, research exploring these issues can lead to more effective policy analysis and assessment, and ultimately to tangible improvements in the character of the decisions reached.

ABBREVIATIONS

BDA	Bangalore Development Authority
BMA	Bangalore Metropolitan Area
DCA	Department of Community Affairs
DDA	Delhi Development Authority
DMA	Delhi Metropolitan Area
DRI	Development of Regional Impact
DUA	Delhi Urban Agglomeration
HUD	U.S. Department of Housing and Urban Development
INR	Indian rupee
IT	Information technology
ITES	Information technology and enabled services
KEONICS	Karnataka State Electronics Development Corporation Limited
KIADB	Karnataka Industrial Areas Development Board
MSA	Metropolitan statistical area
MSCDC	Main South Community Development Corporation
N	Nigerian naira
NCRPB	National Capital Region Planning Board
NCTD	National Capital Territory of Delhi
OSP	Optional Sector Planning
SMSA	Standard metropolitan statistical area
TCPO	Town and Country Planning Organisation
UPP	University Park Partnership

REFERENCES

Acquaye, Emmanuel, and Stephen O. Asiama. 1986. Land policies for housing development for low-income groups in Africa. *Land Development Studies* 3:127–143.

AFCD. *See* Association of Florida Community Developers.

Afshar, Anna. 2005. Community-campus partnerships for economic development: Community perspectives. Public and Community Affairs Discussion Paper 2005-2, Federal Reserve Bank of Boston, Boston, Massachusetts.

Agbola, Tunde. 1990. Affordability and cost recovery in shelter projects: The case of Nigeria. *Third World Planning Review* 12(1):59–74.

Anonymous. 1997. *Market value of land for the purpose of registration around Bangalore as per Karnataka Stamp Act 1957.* Bangalore, India: Sree Ambica Book House.

Association of Florida Community Developers (AFCD). http://www.afcd.com.

Atlas, Terry. 2005. Bangalore's big dreams. *U.S. News & World Report*, May 2, http://www.usnews.com/usnews/biztech/articles/050502/2india.htm.

Avery, Robert B., Raphael W. Bostic, Paul S. Calem, and Glenn B. Canner. 1999. Consolidation and bank branching patterns. *Journal of Banking and Finance* 23 (February):497–532.

Banerji, Manjistha. 2005. *Ensuring public accountability through community action 2005.* New Delhi, India: Institute of Social Studies Trust. Available online at http://www.isst-india.org/public_accountability.htm.

Bangalore Development Authority (BDA). Our mission. http://www.bdaban galore.org/our_mission.html.

———. 1985. *Comprehensive development plan—2001.* Bangalore, India: Bangalore Development Authority.

———. 1995. *Revised comprehensive development plan—2011.* Bangalore, India: Bangalore Development Authority.

———. 2005. *Master plan—2015.* Bangalore, India: Bangalore Development Authority.

Bangalore Metropolitan Regional Development Authority (BMRDA). 2006. *Ban-*

galore Metropolitan Region (BMR) structure plan. Bangalore, India: Bangalore Metropolitan Regional Development Authority.

Bangalore Properties. 2005. IT's on Mysore and Mangalore: Govt. looks at towns as Bangalore hits dead end. http://www.bangaloreproperties.com/it_mysore _mangalore.html.

Barbour, K. Michael, Julius S. Oguntoyinbo, James O. C. Onyemelukwe, and James C. Nwafor. 1982. *Nigeria in maps.* London: Hodder and Stoughton.

Bassett, John. 2005. Campus and community collaboration: First person with John Bassett (interview). *Communities and Banking* 16(2):24–27.

Basu, Kanika, and Laveesh Bhandari. n.d. *The resurgence of urban India: Urban renewal and slum reform for the State of Delhi.* Available online at http:// www.indicus.net.

BBMP. *See* Bruhat Bangalore Mahanagara Palike.

BDA. *See* Bangalore Development Authority.

Ben-Zadok, E. 2005. Consistency, concurrency, and compact development: Three faces of growth management implementation in Florida. *Urban Studies* 42:2167–2190.

Benjamin, Solomon. 2000. Governance, economic settings and poverty in Bangalore. *Environment & Urbanization* 12(1):35–56. Available online at http:// unpan1.un.org/intradoc/groups/public/documents/apcity/unpan020773.pdf.

———. 2006. Inclusive or contested? Conceptualizing a globalized Bangalore— via a closer look at territories of the IT dominated territories in east and south Bangalore. Paper presented at the conference on tackling exclusion: Shelter, basic services, and citizen's rights in globalizing mega cities of Asia, New Delhi, India.

Benjamin, Solomon, R. Bhuvaneswari, P. Rajan, and Manjunath. 2006. "Fractured" terrain, spaces left over, or contested? A closer look at territories of the IT dominated territories in east and south Bangalore. Paper presented at the conference on tackling exclusion: Shelter, basic services, and citizen's rights in globalizing mega cities of Asia, New Delhi, India.

Black, Sandra. 1999. Do better schools matter? Parental valuation of elementary education. *Quarterly Journal of Economics* 14(2):577–599.

BMRDA. *See* Bangalore Metropolitan Regional Development Authority.

Boyle, Melissa A., and Katherine A. Kiel. 2001. A survey of house price hedonic studies of the impact of environmental externalities. *Journal of Real Estate Literature* 9(2):117–144.

Bruhat Bangalore Mahanagara Palike (BBMP). Bengaluru city profile: City summary. http://www.bmponline.org/.

Buchmueller, Thomas C., Mireille Jacobson, and Cheryl Wold. 2004. How far to the hospital? The effect of hospitals on access to care. *Journal of Health Economics* 25 (July):740–761.

Buckley, Robert M., and Jerry Kalarickal. 2005. Housing policy in developing countries: Conjectures and refutations. *World Bank Research Observer* 25:233–257.

BusinessWeek. 2005. Indian land grab. September 19. http://www.businessweek.com/magazine/content/05_38/b3951154.htm.

Calhoun, Charles A. 1996. OFHEO house price indexes: HPI technical description. Paper, Office of Federal Housing Enterprise Oversight, Washington, DC.

Case, Karl, and Robert J. Shiller. 1987. Prices of single family homes since 1970: New indexes for four cities. NBER Working Paper 2393, National Bureau of Economic Research, Cambridge, Massachusetts.

Chapin, Timothy S. 2003. *A population and employment forecast for Franklin County.* Tallahassee, FL: Florida State University Department of Urban and Regional Planning (June).

———. 2007. Not your ordinary Joe: The St. Joe Company and Florida's Great Northwest. Working paper, Lincoln Institute of Land Policy, Cambridge, Massachusetts.

Chapin, Timothy S., Charles Connerly, and Harrison Higgins, eds. 2007. *Growth management in Florida: Planning for paradise.* London: Ashgate Press.

Cheshire, Paul C., and Stephen C. Sheppard. 1995. On the price of land and the value of amenities. *Economica, New Series* 62(246):247–267.

Committee on State Urbanization Policy. 2002. *Proposed state urbanization policy in Karnataka,* part 1. Bangalore, India: Government of Karnataka.

Cousins, Ben, Tessa Cousins, Donna Hornby, Rosalie Kingwill, Lauren Royston, and Warren Smit. 2005. Will formalizing property rights reduce poverty in South Africa's "second economy"? Questioning the mythologies of Hernando De Soto. *PLAAS Policy Brief* 18:1–6.

Cox, David N. 2000. Guest editor's introduction. *Cityscape* 5(1).

Cropper, Maureen L., Leland B. Deck, and Kenneth E. McConnell. 1988. On the choice of functional form for hedonic price functions. *Review of Economics and Statistics* 70(4):668–675.

Dale, Peter. 1997. Land tenure issues in economic development. *Urban Studies* 34:1621–1633.

DCA. *See* Florida Department of Community Affairs.

DDA. *See* Delhi Development Authority.

deAragão, Anamaria, Costa Martins, and Melchior S. Neto. 2007. The impact of university campuses on disperse urban contexts. Working paper, Lincoln Institute of Land Policy, Cambridge, Massachusetts.

Deccan Herald. 2005. IT drives Bangalore office space market: CB Richard Ellis India office market review. November 4. http://www.deccanherald.com/deccanherald/nov42005/realty1833322005113.asp.

DeGrove, John M. 2005. *Planning policy and politics: Smart growth and the states*. Cambridge, MA: Lincoln Institute of Land Policy.

Delhi Development Authority (DDA). a. About us. http://www.dda.org.in/about _us/about_dda.htm.

———. b. Allotment rules. http://www.dda.org.in/assistance/pop_ups/for_allotment.htm.

———. 1981. (Disposal of developed Nazul land) Rules, 1981. GSR 872, dated 26 September. http://www.urbanindia.nic.in/moud/programme/dd/nazul_land .pdf.

———. 2005. *Master plan of Delhi—2021*. See esp. Introduction, Population and employment, and Delhi urban area 2021. Delhi, India: Delhi Development Authority. Available online at http://www.dda.org.in/planning/draft_master_plans.htm.

Delhi Metro Rail Corporation (DMRC). a. Need for a metro. http://www .delhimetrorail.com/corporates/needfor_mrts.html.

———. b. Property development. http://www.delhimetrorail.com/corporates/property_development.html.

Delhi Urban Environment and Infrastructure Improvement Project (DUEIIP). 2001. *Delhi 21*. Delhi, India: Government of India and Government of National Capital Territory of Delhi (January). Available online at http:// delhiplanning.nic.in/Reports/Delhi21/Delhi-21.pdf.

De Soto, Hernando. 2000. *The mystery of capital*. London: Bantam.

DeVol, Ross, Rob Koepp, Perry Wong, and Armen Bedroussian. 2003. *The economic contributions of health care to New England*. Research report prepared for the New England Healthcare Institute. Santa Monica, CA: Milken Institute (February).

Deyle, Robert E., Timothy S. Chapin, and Earl J. Baker. 2007. Are we any safer? An evaluation of Florida's hurricane hazard mitigation planning mandates. In *Growth management in Florida: Planning for paradise*, ed. Timothy S. Chapin, Charles E. Connerly, and Harrison T. Higgins. London: Ashgate Press.

DMRC. *See* Delhi Metro Rail Corporation.

DUEIIP. *See* Delhi Urban Environment and Infrastructure Improvement Project.

Durand-Lasserve, Alain. 1994. Researching the relationship between economic liberalization and changes to land markets and land prices: The case of Conakry, Guinea, 1985–1991. In *Methodology for land and housing market analysis*, ed. Gareth Jones and Peter M. Ward. London: UCL Press.

EPA. *See* U.S. Environmental Protection Agency.

Evans, Alan W. 1999. The land market and government intervention. In *The handbook of regional and urban economics,* ed. Paul Cheshire and Edwin S. Mills. Amsterdam: North-Holland.

Ezeh, Charles F. 1998. Intra-urban migration in Enugu. B.Sc. thesis, Department of Geography, University of Nigeria, Nsukka.

Fannie Mae. 2004. Announcement 04-07. Washington, DC: Fannie Mae (November).

Fischel, William A. 1989. *Do growth controls matter? A review of empirical evidence on the effectiveness and efficiency of local government land use regulation.* Cambridge, MA: Lincoln Institute of Land Policy.

Flores, Glenn, and Sandra C. Tomany-Korman. 2008. Racial and ethnic disparities in medical and dental health, access to care, and use of services in US children. *Pediatrics* 121 (February): e286–e298.

Florida Department of Community Affairs (DCA). 2001. The optional sector plan process. Presentation. Available online at http://www.dca.state.fl.us/fdcp/dcp/optionalsectorplans/files/baycosectorplan.pdf.

———. 2006. Developments of regional impact and Florida quality developments. http://www.dca.state.fl.us/fdcp/DCP/DRIFQD/.

Florida's Great Northwest. http://www.floridasgreatnorthwest.com.

Fogelsong, Richard E. 2001. *Married to the mouse: Walt Disney World and Orlando.* New Haven, CT: Yale University Press.

Freeman, Gregory, Nancy D. Sidhu, and Michael Montoya. 2006. *Hidden in plain sight: The economic contribution of Southern California hospitals and related services.* Los Angeles: Los Angeles County Economic Development Corporation (February).

Frishman, Alan. 1988. The rise of squatting in Kano. In *Slum and squatter settlements in sub-Saharan Africa: Towards a planning strategy,* ed. Robert A. Obudho and Constance C. Mhlanga. New York: Praeger.

Fujita, Masahisha. 1989. *Urban economic theory.* Cambridge, UK: Cambridge University Press.

Gibbons, Steve, and Stephen Machin. 2003. Valuing English primary schools. *Journal of Urban Economics* 53(2):197–219.

Giuliano, Genevieve, and Kenneth A. Small. 1991. Subcenters in the Los Angeles region. *Regional Science and Urban Economics* 21:163–182.

Gladstone, David L. 2005. *From pilgrimage to package tour: Travel and tourism in the third world.* New York and London: Routledge.

Glaeser, Edward L. 2005. Reinventing Boston: 1640–2003. *Journal of Economic Geography* 5(2):119–153.

Gordon, Peter, and Harry W. Richardson. 1997. Are compact cities a desirable planning goal? *Journal of the American Planning Association* 63(1):95–106.

———. 2000. Prove it: The costs and benefits of sprawl. In *Readings in urban eco-*

nomics. Issues and public policy, ed. Robert W. Wassmer. Malden, MA: Blackwell.

Gough, Kate V., and Paul W. K. Yankson. 2000. Land markets in African cities: The case of peri-urban Accra, Ghana. *Urban Studies* 37(13):2485–2500.

Government of Anambra State. 1978. A *Comprehensive physical development plan for Enugu.* Enugu, Nigeria: Government Press.

Government of National Capital Territory of Delhi (NCTD). 2005a. *Annual plan: 2005–2006.* See esp. vol. 4, sec. 2, Housing. Available online at http://delhiplanning.nic.in/write-up/2005-06/Volume-4/housing.pdf.

———. 2005b. *Annual plan: 2005–2006.* See esp. vol. 4, sec. 2, Urban development. Available online at http://delhiplanning.nic.in/write-up/2005-06/Volume-4/ud.pdf.

———. 2005c. *Economic survey of Delhi 2003–2004.* See esp. chap. 14, Urban development. Available online at http://delhiplanning.nic.in/Economic%20Survey/Ecosur2003-04/Ch14.pdf.

Henderson, J. Vernon. 1988. *Urban development: Theory, fact and illusion.* Oxford: Oxford University Press.

HUD. *See* U.S. Department of Housing and Urban Development.

Hussain, Mohammed. 2004. Unauthorised developments—problems. *Real Estate Reporter* 12(4):17–19.

———. 2006. Residential areas and housing situation in Bangalore. *Real Estate Reporter* 6(1):6–8.

ICIC. *See* Initiative for a Competitive Inner City.

Ikejiofor, Cosmas U. 1997. The private sector and urban housing production process in Nigeria: A study of small scale landlords in Abuja. *Habitat International* 21(4):409–425.

———. 2006. Equity in informal land delivery: Insights from Enugu, Nigeria. *Land Use Policy* 23(4):448–459.

———. 2007. The impact of customary landholding on emerging land markets in Enugu, Nigeria. Working paper, Lincoln Institute of Land Policy, Cambridge, Massachusetts.

Ikejiofor, Cosmas U., with Kenneth C. Nwogu and Cyril O. Nwanunobi. 2004. Informal land delivery processes and access to land for the poor in Enugu, Nigeria. Working paper, University of Birmingham, School of Public Policy, International Development Department, Birmingham, UK.

———. 2002b. Census of India: 2001 (provisional). Subjects. http://www.censusindia.net/results/popul.html.

Initiative for a Competitive Inner City (ICIC) and CEOs for Cities. 2002. *Leveraging colleges and universities for urban economic revitalization: An action agenda.* New York: ICIC and CEOs for Cities.

Jacobs, Jane. 1961. *The death and life of great American cities*. New York: Vintage Press.

———. 1969. *The economy of cities*. New York: John Wiley.

Jehl, Douglas. 2002. Vast change looms for Florida timber tracts. *New York Times*, June 22.

Kamala, A. 2003. Bangalore realty sector buoyant. *Real Estate Reporter* 3(8):12–15.

Karnataka Industrial Areas Development Board (KIADB). n.d. Procedure for allotment of land.

———. 2006a. Industrial area wise land acquired, developed and allotted as on 30-6-2006. Bangalore, India: KIADB.

———. 2006b. Database of industrial areas (electronic file). Bangalore, India: Karnataka Industrial Areas Development Board.

Karnataka Slum Clearance Board (KSCB). 2006a. Abstract: Statement showing the declared slum list in Bangalore city. Bangalore, India: Karnataka Slum Clearance Board.

———. 2006b. Vambay houses taken under phase-I, phase-II (1st half) & phase-III (1st half and 2nd half). Bangalore, India: Karnataka Slum Clearance Board.

Kelly, Eric Damian, and Barbara Becker. 2000. *Community planning: An introduction to the comprehensive plan*. Washington, DC: Island Press.

KIADB. *See* Karnataka Industrial Areas Development Board.

Kodandapani, A. S. 2005a. Comprehensive development plan 2015. *Real Estate Reporter* 5(2):20–21.

———. 2005b. Implications of information technology activity in Bangalore. *Real Estate Reporter* 5(3):22–23.

———. 2005c. Unauthorised developments. *Real Estate Reporter* 5(4):6–8.

Krugman, Paul R. 1991. *Geography and trade*. Cambridge, MA: MIT Press.

KSCB. *See* Karnataka Slum Clearance Board.

Kumar, Narendra. 2003. Land development process in fringe areas of Delhi: Case study of Gurgaon and Ghaziabad. Master's dissertation, Center for Environmental Planning and Technology, School of Planning, Ahmedabad, Gujarat, India.

Kumar, Sunil. 2001. *Social relations, rental housing markets & the poor in urban India*. Final report to the Infrastructure & Urban Development Department, Department for International Development (DFID). London: London School of Economics & Political Science (September). Available online at http://www.worldbank.org/html/fpd/urban/poverty/docs/social-relation-kumar.pdf.

Kundu, Amitabh. 2003. Politics and economics of land policies: Delhi Master Plan 2001 [electronic version]. *Economic and Political Weekly*, August 23. Available online at http://www.epw.org.in/showindex.php.

Kundu, Debolina, and Amitabh Kundu. 2006. Urban land market, tenurial security, and the poor: An overview of policies with special reference to Delhi. Paper presented at the conference on tackling exclusion: Shelter, basic services and citizen's rights in globalizing mega cities of Asia, New Delhi, India. Available online at http://www.fig.net/commission7/bangkok_2005/papers/7_3_kundu_amit.pdf.

Lateef, Asma. 1997. *Linking up with the global economy: A case study of the Bangalore software industry.* Geneva, Switzerland: International Institute for Labour Studies, International Labour Organization. Available online at http://www.ilo.org/public/english/bureau/inst/papers/1997/dp96/index.htm.

Logan, John R., and Harvey L. Molotch. 1987. *Urban fortunes: The political economy of place.* Berkeley, CA: University of California Press.

Mabogunje, Akin L. 1992. Perspectives on urban land and urban land management policies in sub-Saharan Africa. Technical Paper 196, World Bank, Washington, DC.

Mahadevia, Darshini. 2006. Metropolitan employment in India. Paper presented at the conference on tackling exclusion: Shelter, basic services, and citizen's rights in globalizing mega cities of Asia, New Delhi, India.

Malpani, Juhi. 2003. Urban governance in national capital territory of Delhi: A study of development parameters in the planning, municipal administrative process. Master's dissertation, Center for Environmental Planning and Technology, School of Planning, Ahmedabad, Gujarat, India.

Mbiba, Beacon, and Marie Huchzermeyer. 2002. Contentious development: Peri-urban studies in sub-Saharan Africa. *Progress in Development Studies* 2(2):113–131.

McAuslan, Patrick. 1998. Making law work: Restructuring land reforms in Africa. *Development and Change* 29(3):193–204.

McConnell, Virginia, and Margaret Walls. 2005. The value of open space: Evidence from studies of nonmarket benefits. Working paper, Lincoln Institute of Land Policy, Cambridge, Massachusetts.

McMillen, Daniel. 2001. Nonparametric employment subcenter identification. *Journal of Urban Economics* 50(3):448–473.

Melnick, Glenn A., Amar Nawathe, Anil Bamezai, and Lois Green. 2004. Emergency department capacity and access in California, 1990–2001: An economic analysis. *Health Affairs*, March. http://content.healthaffairs.org/cgi/content/full/hlthaff.w4.136v1/DC1.

Mills, Edwin S. 1967. An aggregative model of resource allocation in a metropolitan area. *American Economic Review* 57:197–210.

———. 1972. *Urban economics.* Glenview, IL: Scott Foresman.

Ministry of Urban Development (MoUD), Government of India. http://urbanindia.nic.in/moud/theministry/statutorynautonomous/dda/main.htm.

Mitra, Sanjay. 2002. Planned urbanisation through public participation: Case of the new town, Kolkata. *Economic and Political Weekly* 37(11):1048–1054.

Molinsky, Jennifer H. 2006. Landowners on the metropolitan fringe: Results from a survey of owners in four U.S. metropolitan areas. Working paper, Lincoln Institute of Land Policy, Cambridge, Massachusetts.

Mookherjee, Debnath, and Eugene Hoerauf. 2004. Cities in transition: Monitoring growth trends in Delhi Urban Agglomeration: 1991–2001. In *Cities in transition*, ed. M. Pak and D. Rebernik. Ljubljana, Slovenia: University of Ljubljana. Available online at http://www.ff.uni-lj.si/oddelki/geo/publikacije/dela/files/dela_21/020%20mookherjee.pdf.

MoUD. *See* Indian Ministry of Urban Development.

Muth, Richard F. 1969. *Cities and housing: The spatial pattern of urban residential land use.* Chicago: University of Chicago Press.

Nagarajan, Rema. 2006. Bangalore: The best place to live in India. *Times of India*, September 4. http://timesofindia.indiatimes.com/articleshow/msid-1953010,curpg-1.cms.

Nair, Janaki. 2005. *The promise of the metropolis: Bangalore's twentieth century.* New Delhi, India: Oxford University Press.

National Capital Regional Planning Board (NCRPB). 1999a. *Delhi: A fact sheet.* New Delhi, India: National Capital Region Planning Board.

———. 1999b. *National capital region growth & development.* New Delhi, India: Har-Anand.

———. 2005. *Regional plan—2021: National Capital Region.* New Delhi, India: National Capital Regional Planning Board.

NCRPB. *See* National Capital Regional Planning Board.

NCTD. *See* Government of National Capital Territory of Delhi.

NDMC. *See* New Delhi Municipal Council.

New Delhi Municipal Council (NDMC). 2005. New Delhi Municipal Council Act, 1994: Introduction. http://www.ndmc.gov.in/AboutNDMC/NNDMCAct.aspx.

Office of the Registrar General and Census Commissioner, India. 2002a. Census of India: 2001 (provisional). Rural-urban population: Indian states and union territories. http://www.censusindia.net/results/rudist.html.

Okolocha, Chike F. 1993. The evolution of a land policy. In *Urban development in Nigeria: Planning, housing, and land policy*, ed. Richard W. Taylor. Aldershot, UK: Avebury.

Olima, Washington H. A., and Volker Kreibich. 2002. Land management for rapid urbanization under poverty: An introduction. In *Urban land management in Africa*, ed. Volker Kreibich and Washington H. A. Olima. Spring Research Series 40. Dortmund, Germany: University of Dortmund, Faculty of Spatial Planning.

Olsen, Edgar O. 1999. The demand and supply of housing service: A critical survey of the empirical literature. In *The handbook of regional and urban economics*, ed. Paul Cheshire and Edwin S. Mills. Amsterdam: North-Holland.

Payne, Geoffrey K. 1997. *Urban land tenure and property rights in developing countries: A review*. London: IT Publications/ODA.

Perry, David C., and Wim Wiewel. 2005. *The university as urban developer: Case studies and analysis*. Armonk, NY: M. E. Sharpe.

Porter, Michael E. 1990. *The competitive advantage of nations*. New York: Free Press.

Puliani, S. 2005. *Estimated market value of the immovable properties and buildings for registration in Bangalore (urban) district*. Bangalore, India: Karnataka Law Journal Publications.

Rajya Sabha. 2005. Synopsis of debates (proceedings other than questions and answers), Thursday, March 24, 2005/Chaitra 3, 1927 (Saka), Matters raised with permission of chair. http://164.100.24.167/rsdebate/synopsis/204/24032005.htm.

Rakodi, Carole. 2006. Social agency and state authority in land delivery processes in African cities: Compliance, conflict and cooperation. *International Development Planning Review* 28(2):263–285.

Redfearn, Christian L. 2007. The topography of metropolitan employment: Identifying centers of employment in a polycentric urban area. *Journal of Urban Economics* 61(3):519–541.

Rosen, Sherwin. 1974. Hedonic prices and implicit markets: Product differentiation in pure competition. *Journal of Political Economy* 82(1):34–55.

Royston, Lauren, Tessa Cousins, Donna Hornby, Rosalie Kingwell, and Thelma Trench. 2005. Perspectives on land tenure security in rural and urban South Africa: An analysis of tenure context and a problem statement for LEAP. Commissioned paper, Legal Entity Assessment Project (LEAP), KwaZulu Natal, South Africa.

Rubin, V. 2000. Evaluating university-community partnerships: An examination of the evolution of questions and approaches. *Cityscape* 3(1):219–230.

Savitch, Hank V., and Paul Kantor. 2002. *Cities in the international marketplace*. Princeton, NJ: Princeton University Press.

Scheffler, Richard, Rachael Kagan, Lisa S. Maiuro, Julie Schmittdiel, and Wil Yu. 2001. *California's closed hospitals, 1995–2000*. Berkeley, CA: Nicholas C. Petris Center on Health Care Markets and Consumer Welfare, University of California, Berkeley, School of Public Health (April).

Schwartz, Amy E., Scott Susin, and Ioan Voicu. 2003. Has falling crime driven New York City's real estate boom? *Journal of Housing Research* 14(1):101–135.

Siemiatycki, Matti. 2006. Message in a metro: Building urban rail infrastructure and image in Delhi, India. *International Journal of Urban and Regional Research* 30(2):277–292.

Simha, R. N. 1999. *Latest market value of land for the purpose of registration around Bangalore as per Karnataka Stamp Act 1957.* Bangalore, India: Sree Ambica Book House.

———. 2001. *Latest market value of land for the purpose of registration around Bangalore as per Karnataka Stamp Act 1957.* Bangalore: Sree Ambica Book House.

Simon, David. 1992. *Cities, capital and development: African cities in the world economy.* London: Belhaven Press.

Singh, Mahendra Kumar. 2007. Plan to shrink Delhi's VIP zone. *Times of India.* November 1. http://timesofindia.indiatimes.com/articleshow/2506957.cms.

Sita, K., and M. Chatterjee. 1990. Metropolitan dominance in India: The demographic imprint of colonial dependency. In *Cities and development in the third world,* ed. R. B. Potter and A. T. Salau. London: Mansell.

Sivam, Alpana. 2003. Housing supply in Delhi. *Cities* 20:135–141.

Smolka, Martim O. 2003. Informality, urban poverty and land market prices. *Land Lines* (January):4–7.

Space Daily. 2004. Outsourcing firms gobble up farm land to meet space demand in India. February 29. http://www.spacedaily.com/2004/040229030445.ubh9vxdw.html.

Srirangan, K. 2000. Public land and property development and cross-subsidisation for low-income housing in Delhi. App. 1 of *Delhi field studies and workshop: Guide to good practice in core area development.* DFID Research Project R6860. London: Max Lock Centre, University of Westminster (March). Available online at http://www.wmin.ac.uk/builtenv/maxlock/Core_Areas/Studies/Delhi/18_App_I.pdf.

St. Joe Company. 2005. The St. Joe Company (NYSE: JOE) outlines vision for "new ruralism." News release, June 4. http://ir.joe.com/releasedetail.cfm?releaseid=194026.

———. 2006. *St. Joe Company 2005 annual report.* http://ir.joe.com/annuals.cfm?Year=2005.

TCPO. *See* Town and Country Planning Organisation.

Tejendra Khanna Committee. 2006. *Report of the Tejendra Khanna Committee of India to look into various aspects of unauthorized constructions & misuse of premises in Delhi.* New Delhi, India: Akalank Publications (May).

Times of India. 2005a. Delhi-Gurgaon highway zipping into 2006. June 15. http://timesofindia.indiatimes.com/articleshow/1143201.cms.

———. 2005b. Exit Bangalore, enter Bengaluru, Kolkata, Mumbai, Chennai. December 11. http://timesofindia.indiatimes.com/articleshow/1327480.cms.

——. 2007a. Delhi needs full statehood: Dikshit. November 23. http://timesof
india.indiatimes.com/articleshow/2564966.cms.

——. 2007b. World suffers from "Bangalore envy." January 9. http://timesof
india.indiatimes.com/Bangalore_envy_hits_world/articleshow/1101456.cms.

Town and Country Planning Organisation (TCPO). 1995. *Appraisal of land policies and programmes: A case study of Delhi, Ghaziabad and Noida.* New
Delhi, India: Ministry of Urban Affairs and Employment.

UNCHS. *See* United Nations Centre for Human Settlements.

United Nations Centre for Human Settlements (UNCHS). 1996. *An urbanizing
world: Global report on human settlements 1996.* New York: Oxford University Press.

——. 2001. *Cities in a globalizing world: Global report on human settlements
2001.* London: Earthscan.

U.S. Department of Housing and Urban Development (HUD). 2003. Mortgagee
Letter 2003–07. Washington, DC: U.S. Department of Housing and Urban
Development (May).

——. 2005. Office of Policy Development and Research. *The power of partnership: Celebrating 10 years.* Washington, DC: U.S. Department of Housing
and Urban Development.

U.S. Environmental Protection Agency (EPA). Gardner-Kilby-Hammond (GKH)
revitalization project. http://www.epa.gov/region01/brownfields/success/06/
gkhrp_worcester_ma_ag_cg.htm.

Vagale, L. R. 2002. From Silicon Valley to garbage city. *Real Estate Reporter*
2(9):22–24.

Van Westen, A. C. M. 1990. Land supply for low income housing, Bamako, Mali:
Its evolution and performance. In *The transformation of land supply systems
in third world cities,* ed. Paul Baross and Jan van der Linden. Aldershot, UK:
Avebury.

Vidal, Avis, Nancy Nye, Christopher Waler, Carlos Manjarrez, and Clare
Romanik. 2002. *Lessons from the Community Outreach Partnership Center
Program.* Report prepared for the U.S. Department of Housing and Urban
Development. Washington, DC: Urban Institute (March).

Warner, Kee, and Harvey Molotch. 2001. *Building rules: How local controls shape
community environments and economies.* Boulder, CO: Westview.

Weiss, Marc A. 1987. *The rise of the community builders: The American real estate
industry and urban land planning.* New York: Columbia University Press.

Wheeler, Stephen M. 2002. The new regionalism: Characteristics of an emerging movement. *Journal of the American Planning Association* 68:267–278.

Wiewel, Wim, and Gerrit Knapp. 2005. *Partnerships for smart growth: University-
community collaboration for better public places.* Armonk, NY: M. E. Sharpe.

World Bank. 1996. *Restoring urban Nigeria.* Lagos, Nigeria: World Bank.

Zabel, Jeffery E. 1999. Controlling for quality in house price indices. *Journal of Real Estate Finance and Economics* 19(3):223–241.

Ziewitz, Kathryn, and June M. Wiaz. 2004. *Green empire: The St. Joe Company and the remaking of Florida's panhandle*. Gainesville, FL: University Press of Florida.

CONTRIBUTORS

EDITOR

RAPHAEL W. BOSTIC
Professor
School of Policy, Planning, and Development
University of Southern California

AUTHORS

JOHN C. BROWN
Professor
Department of Economics
Clark University

TIMOTHY S. CHAPIN
Department Chair and Associate Professor
Department of Urban and Regional Planning
Florida State University

JACQUELINE GEOGHEGAN
Associate Professor
Department of Economics
Clark University

DAVID L. GLADSTONE
Associate Professor
Department of Planning and Urban Studies
University of New Orleans

(continued)

COSMAS UCHENNA IKEJIOFOR
Adjunct Associate Professor of Urban and Regional Planning
Caritas University
Enugu, Nigeria; and
Chief Architect
Federal Ministry of Environment, Housing, and Urban Development
Field Headquarters
Ebonyi State, Nigeria

KAMESWARA SREENIVAS KOLAPALLI
Ph.D. student
Department of Planning and Urban Studies
University of New Orleans

LaVONNA B. LEWIS
Clinical Associate Professor
School of Policy, Planning, and Development
University of Southern California

DAVID C. SLOANE
Professor
School of Policy, Planning, and Development
University of Southern California

PENGYU ZHU
Ph.D. student
School of Policy, Planning, and Development
University of Southern California

INDEX

Page numbers with a t *and an* f *indicate a table and a figure, respectively.*

ABOUT THE LINCOLN INSTITUTE
OF LAND POLICY

The Lincoln Institute of Land Policy is a private operating foundation whose mission is to improve the quality of public debate and decisions in the areas of land policy and land-related taxation in the United States and around the world. The Institute's goals are to integrate theory and practice to better shape land policy and to provide a nonpartisan forum for discussion of the multidisciplinary forces that influence public policy. This focus on land derives from the Institute's founding objective—to address the links between land policy and social and economic progress—that was identified and analyzed by political economist and author Henry George.

The work of the Institute is organized in three departments: Valuation and Taxation, Planning and Urban Form, and International Studies, which includes programs on Latin America and China. We seek to inform decision making through education, research, demonstration projects, and the dissemination of information through publications, our Web site, and other media. Our programs bring together scholars, practitioners, public officials, policy advisers, and involved citizens in a collegial learning environment. The Institute does not take a particular point of view, but rather serves as a catalyst to facilitate analysis and discussion of land use and taxation issues—to make a difference today and to help policy makers plan for tomorrow. The Lincoln Institute of Land Policy is an equal opportunity institution.

L LINCOLN INSTITUTE
OF LAND POLICY
CAMBRIDGE, MASSACHUSETTS

113 Brattle Street
Cambridge, MA 02138-3400 USA
Phone: 1-617-661-3016 x127 or 1-800-526-3873
Fax: 1-617-661-7235 or 1-800-526-3944
E-mail: help@lincolninst.edu
Web: www.lincolninst.edu